英文

# 日本絵とき事典6

## ILLUSTRATED
# MUST-SEE IN NIKKO

[日光編]

D0897329

*ILLUSTRATED*

MUST-SEE IN NIKKO

© 1991 by Japan Travel Bureau, Inc.
All rights reserved.

1st edition . . . . . . . 1985
3rd edition . . . . . . 1991

Printed in Japan

---

**About this Book**

1) Layout

   This book consists of three main sections corresponding to the following three areas of Nikko: 1)
Nikko Sannai; 2) Oku-Nikko; 3) Mashiko, Yūki and
Karasuyama. The Nikko Sannai section has a special
subsection on Tōshōgū Shrine. The locations of the
temples, shrines and other sights described in the book
can be found on the appropriate area map at the beginning of each section. The special names and terms
marked with an asterisk are explained in the glossary
at the end of the book.

2) Japanese Words

   All the Japanese words in this book have been
romanized in accordance with the revised Hepburn
system. Except for the names of places and people, all
Japanese words are printed in italics except where
they appear in headings or bold type. Long vowels are
indicated by a line above, as in *shintō* and, since e's are
pronounced "ay" in Japanese, e's at the ends of words
are marked with an acute accent, as in *saké* (pronounced "sahkay").

*Dear Readers*

●

Nikko, besides being one of the most famous sightseeing areas in Japan, has since ancient times been an important center for the religion known as sangaku shinkō, or mountain worship. The mountains in the area have always been revered and feared as the home of gods and demons, and some of the most important shrines and temples in Japan have been built here. Among these is Tōshōgū Shrine, the magnificent mausoleum of the most famous of the shōgun, Tokugawa Ieyasu.

Nikko is an area of outstanding natural beauty, and its shrines and temples are unique examples of traditional Japanese culture, history and religion. No traveler to Japan should miss the experience of a visit here; and this book, the sixth in the "Japan in Your Pocket" series, is designed to make such a visit doubly enjoyable and rewarding.

Route 401

Konsei Pass

Route 120

Mt. Tarō

Mt. Nyohō

Kinugawa-onsen

Shi...ujiwa

Kirifuri Heights

Mt. Shirane

Mt. Ōmanago

NIKKO SANNAI

OKU-NIKKO (p.128)

Tōbu-Nikko (p.11)

Senjō-ga-hara

Mt. Nantai

Gumma Pref.

Lake Chūzenji

Nikko

Shimo-ima

Imaichi

Route 122

Ro...

Mt. Kōkai

Shimozuke-ōsawa

Fubasami

Matō

JR Nik...

Mt. Kōshin

Tsūdō

Ashio

Route 352

Tōbu Nikko Line

Haramukō

Mt. Kesamaru

Watarase Keikoku Tetsudō

So-ori

Shin-kanuma

Konaka

Gōdo

Hanawa

River Watarase

Tochigi Pref.

Kami-kambai

Ōmama

Nishi-kiryū

Kiryū

Aioi

Route 293

Iwajuku

Kuzu-u

Shin-tochigi

Tochigi

Omata

Tanuma

Ōhirashita

Yamamae

Ashikaga

Tomita

Iwafune

Shin-ōhirash...

Ashikaga-shi

Sano

Tōbu Sano Line

Sakai-machi

Ōta

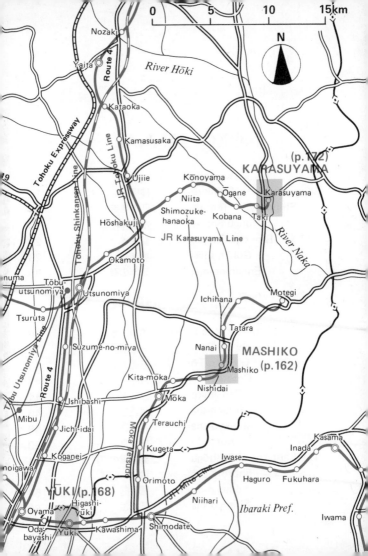

# CONTENTS

## NIKKO SANNAI

## TŌSHŌGŪ SHRINE

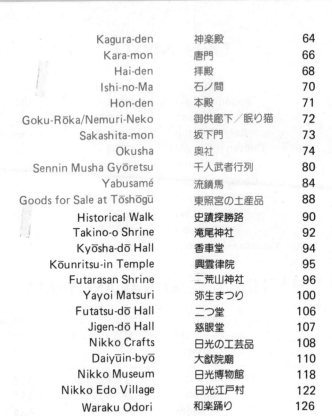

# OKU NIKKO

# MASHIKO/YŪKI/KARASUYAMA

## FEATURE PAGES

## Key to Symbols

Tōshōgū   Shrines   Temples   Festivals   Other

 Buildings other than Temples and Shrines

 Other Sight-seeing Spots

● For words or items marked with *, see GROSSARY starting on p.180 for detailed descriptions.

# ≪  SEE NIKKO WITH JTB'S SUNRISE TOURS  ≫

The Japan Travel Bureau's Sunrise Tours are specially designed with the foreign visitor in mind. Tours lasting from one day to two weeks are available to all the most interesting parts of Japan. Those which include Nikko in their itineraries are described below.

* **Nikko Full-Day Tour**

    Tōshōgū Shrine, Futarasan Shrine (with sacred dance performance), Iroha-zaka Hill, Kegon Falls, Lake Chūzenji, Chūzen-ji Temple.
    From Tokyo (Asakusa) to Nikko by special express train.
    ¥ 18,500

* **Nikko 2-Day Tour**

    Tōshōgū Shrine, Futarasan Shrine (with sacred dance performance), Iroha-zaka Hill, Kegon Falls, Lake Chūzenji, Chūzen-ji Temple.
    From Tokyo (Asakusa) to Nikko by special express train.
    ¥ 28,000

* **Nikko Spring Grand Festival Tour**

    May 18
    ¥ 19,500

* **Nikko Autumn Grand Festival Tour**

    Oct. 17
    ¥ 19,500

The above two tours include the spring or autumn festivals held at Tōshōgū Shrine, and the *Sennin Musha Gyōretsu* (Parade of a Thousand Warriors).

| Notes | |
|---|---|
| | * Tours depart every day. |
| | * Pickup and return area by special Sunrise Bus from your hotel lobby. |
| | * The above prices are adult prices for standard tours. Deluxe tours are also available at special prices. |
| | * The above information is effective as of 1991. |
| | * For bookings and information, contact: Tokyo (03)3276-7777 |

# NIKKO SANNAI

Nikko Sannai, at the center of the Nikko mountain area,
has 57 shrines and temples
including Tōshōgū Shrine, Rinnō-ji Temple,
and Futarasan Shrine.
Most of these are extremely important examples of
Japanese history and culture,
and are visited by huge numbers of tourists every year.

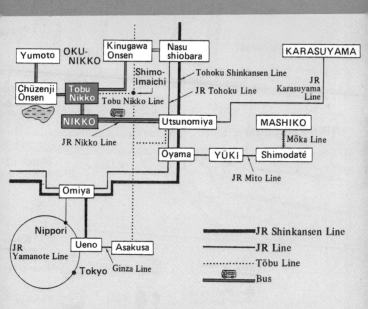

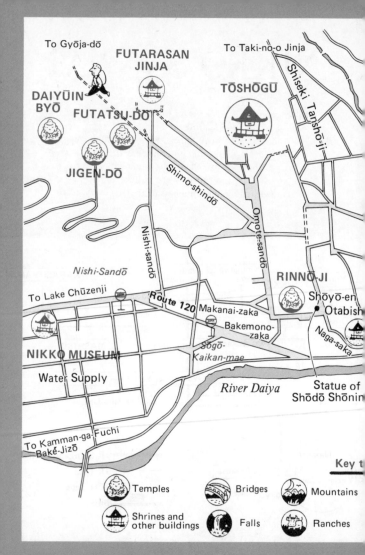

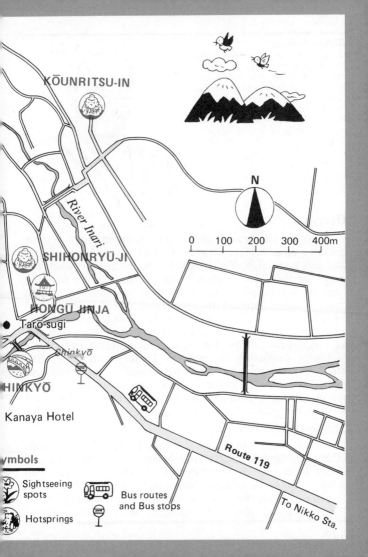

KŌUNRITSU-IN

River Inari

SHIHONRYŪ-JI

HONGŪ JINJA

● Taro-sugi

Shinkyō

SHINKYŌ

Kanaya Hotel

N

0    100    200    300    400m

Route 119

To Nikko Sta.

ymbols

Sightseeing
spots

Bus routes
and Bus stops

Hotsprings

## Shōdō Shōnin

In 766, the high priest Shōdō Shōnin climbed the hitherto untrodden mountains of Nikko and founded the temple Shihonryū-ji, following this by establishing Hongū Shrine, part of the present Futarasan Shrine complex, in 767, and Chūzen-ji Temple in 784.

## Overview

Nikko has been a center for mountain worship since ancient times, and has always been feared as the home of gods and supernatural beings. Its history began in 766, when the priest Shōdō Shōnin climbed the mountains of Nikko and built Shihonryū-ji Temple to the gods of the mountains. Since that time, Tōshōgū Shrine, Futarasan Shrine, Rinnō-ji Temple and 54 other shrines and temples have been built here, making the area one of Japan's most important religious centers. It is also an unparalleled sightseeing area, with its shrine and temple buildings, displaying the peak of Japanese arts and crafts, blending harmoniously with the beautiful and mysterious natural scenery. The charm of Nikko, a place which brings the visitor into close contact with Japanese history, culture and religion, is undiminished even today.

## Shimbutsu Shūgō

The religion of Nikko is unique in celebrating the gods of *Shintō,* Japan's indigenous religion, and Buddhism, introduced from abroad, simultaneously in the same place. This religion, called *Shimbutsu Shūgō* (combined Shintoism and Buddhism) holds that Buddha appears to save mankind in the form of *Shintō* gods called *Gongen.* Most of the religious

**Cedar Avenue**

The road to Nikko is lined on both sides with huge *sugi* (Japanese cedars) more than three hundred years old, creating a deep and mysterious atmosphere. These trees are said to number approximately 14,000.

buildings at Nikko are combinations of shrine and temple architecture, and are divided into those dedicated to *Gongen* and those dedicated to Buddha.

## Nikko Sansha Gongen

The *Nikko Sansha Gongen* are the three *Gongen* believed to reside at Nikko, one on Mt. Nantai, one on Mt. Nyohō, and one on Mt. Tarō. They are also thought to be altered forms of the three Buddhas Batō Kannon, Amida Nyorai and Senju Kannon, enshrined in the Sambutsu-dō Hall of Rinnō-ji Temple.

## Shintoism and Buddhism

The relation between Shintoism and Buddhism is extremely complex. Shintoism teaches that mountains, seas and all natural things are gods, and that the Emperor of Japan is descended from the sun god, *Amaterasu Ōmikami.* This is why the Emperor was historically regarded as a living god. However, *Shintō* enjoyed only a brief spell as the national religion, and Buddhism was the predominant religion from the 7th century to the 19th century, when political power was restored to the Emperor. The two religions have thus existed side-by-side, with many Japanese praying to the *Shintō* gods for material blessings and to Buddha for happiness in the after-life. *Shimbutsu Shūgō* developed as a way of reconciling the differences between the two religions.

◆神橋

# SHINKYŌ

The Shinkyō, or Sacred Bridge, is a beautiful red-lacquered bridge crossing the river Daiya at the entrance to the Nikko Mountain area. The bridge used to be known as Yamasugé-no-Jabashi (Bridge of Snakes with Wild Sedges), after a legend concerning the priest Shōdō Shōnin. It was constructed in its present form in 1636 and became known as Shinkyō because of its outstanding beauty. Except at special religious èvents, only the *shōgun* and the Emperor or members of their retinue were allowed to cross it.

**Oyabashira**
There are two *oyabashira* (large pillars) at the center of the bridge and four at each bank. The head of each pillar is decorated with a knob called a *giboshi* in the shape of a leek.

The handrails are beautifully decorated with golden metal fittings.

The bridge is 27-m-long, 6-m-wide and 16-m above the surface of the water, and is supported by stone pillars.

Anyone crossing the bridge (bridge = *hashi* in Japanese) at festivals receives a commemorative pair of chopsticks (also called *hashi* in Japanese).

### Gejō Ishi

In front of the shinkyō is a special stone called Gejō Ishi. *Gejō* means to dismount, and this stone signifies that all visitors to the holy area that is Nikko must dismount from their horses or alight from their vehicles before crossing the Shinkyō bridge.

### Legend of Yamasugé-no-Jabashi Bridge

When Shōdō Shōnin and ten of his disciples attempted to explore the Nikko mountain area in 767, they were halted by the River Daiya. The current was strong and there was no bridge by which to cross. Shōdō Shōnin began to pray fervently, and his prayers were answered by the god Jinja Daiō, who appeared carrying a red and a blue snakes. He threw these across the river, and they twined together, forming a bridge. The snakes had *yamasugé* (wild sedges) growing from their backs, enabling Shōdō Shōnin and his party to cross without slipping. When the bridge was built, it was called Yamasugé-no-Jabashi (Bridge of Snakes with Wild Sedges) in honor of Jinja-Daiō.

# SHIHONRYŪ-JI TEMPLE

Shihonryū-ji Temple, part of the Rinnō-ji Temple complex, was originally a small retreat built by Shōdō Shōnin after he had observed a mysterious purple cloud forming over the spot. This was the first structure to be built at Nikko. It was subsequently enlarged, but the only original buildings remaining now are the Kannon-dō Hall and the Sanjū-no-Tō.

## Kannon-dō Hall

Named after its patron saint, *Senju Kannon,* this *shiraki*-style (unpainted) cedar hall was built in 807.

## Shiunseki

This 1-m-diameter flat stone in front of the Sanjū-no-Tō commemorates the purple cloud seen by Shōdō Shōnin. The cloud is said to have risen from the spot marked by the stone and drifted away towards Mt. Futara (Mt. Nantai).

## Sanjū-no-Tō (Three-Storied Pagoda)

This 6-m-square, red-lacquered pagoda was built in the 13th century. The twelve animals of the *jūnishi* (the Chinese Zodiac) are carved of the *kaerumata** of the bottom storey.

◆本宮神社

# HONGŪ SHRINE

Hongū Shrine, part of the present Futarasan Shrine complex, was built in 767 by Shōdō Shōnin in thanks to the gods of Mt. Futara (Mt. Nantai) after he had succeeded in climbing this mountain. Later, the enshrinement of Mt. Futara was taken over by Shingū, of Main Shrine (see p. 96), and Hongū Shrine was dedicated to the gods of Mt. Tarō.

In the back of the main hall of Hongū Shrine is a door which opens to reveal holy Mt. Nantai, a reminder of the cult of mountain worship.

Hongū Shrine and Shihonryū-ji Temple, both of which are located in the mountains facing Nikko Bridge, are together with Shinkyō Bridge, important relics from the earliest period of Nikko's history.

### Shūgaku Ryokō

In spring and autumn, specially-chartered coaches arrive at Nikko to deposit hordes of uniformed, camera-toting school pupils on the school study trips known as *shūgaku ryokō*. These outings are held to mark the third and final year of junior or senior high school. Many of the students try to engage foreign tourists in conversation to test whether the English they have learnt in school actually works.

How do you do.

◆輪王寺

# RINNŌ-JI TEMPLE

In the 17th century, Shihonryū-ji Temple, founded by the high priest Shōdō Shōnin (see p.14) in 766, developed into the huge temple complex known as Rinnō-ji. The head temple of the Tendai-shū* Sect, this complex consists of one main temple and 15 *tatchū* (minor temples), and boasts a large congregation of followers.

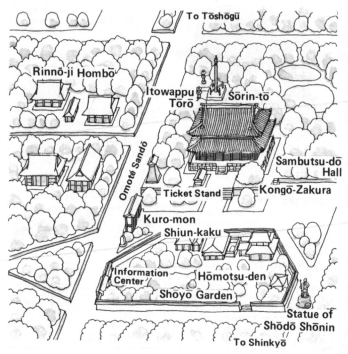

To Tōshōgū

Rinnō-ji Hombō

Itowappu Tōrō

Sōrin-tō

Omote Sandō

Sambutsu-dō Hall

Ticket Stand

Kongō-Zakura

Kuro-mon

Shiun-kaku

Information Center

Hōmotsu-den

Shōyō Garden

Statue of Shōdō Shōnin

To Shinkyō

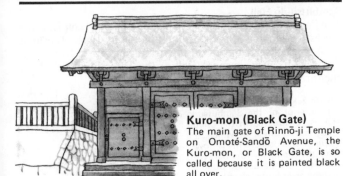

## Kuro-mon (Black Gate)

The main gate of Rinnō-ji Temple on Omoté-Sandō Avenue, the Kuro-mon, or Black Gate, is so called because it is painted black all over.

## Kongō-Zakura

This old cherry tree in front of the Sambutsu-dō Hall is a rare species of *Ōyama-zakura*. Its trunk has a circumference of 5-m and is split into tour at the base. Every year at the beginning of May, it is covered with sweet-scented white blossoms.

**Jikaku-Daishi** (794 — 864)

This Heian-Era high priest became head of the Tendai-shū Sect in 854. He built Rinnō-ji Temple's Sambutsu-dō, Jōgyō-dō and Hokké-dō Halls, and passed on the tradition of the Ennen-no-Mai dance (see p. 30).

**Jigen-Daishi** (1536 — 1643)

This high priest of the early Edo Era became head priest of Mt. Nikko in 1613 and was entrusted by Tokugawa Ieyasu with the task of rebuilding the temple buildings destroyed in the civil wars.

## Sambutsu-dō Hall

The Sambutsu-dō Hall, the main hall of Rinnō-ji Temple, is the biggest building at Mt. Nikkō. Built in 848 by Jikaku Daishi, it is 26.6-m-tall, 32.7-m-wide at the front, and 25.5 m from front to back. Its name means "Hall of the Three Buddhas", after the three statues of Buddha kept inside it.

### Chūdō-zukuri

The interior of the Sambutsudō Hall is constructed in the *Chūdō* style, a rare style in which the *naijin* (inner sanctum) is lower than the *shumidan* (the dais with the altar and statues of Buddha) and the *gejin* (outer chamber).

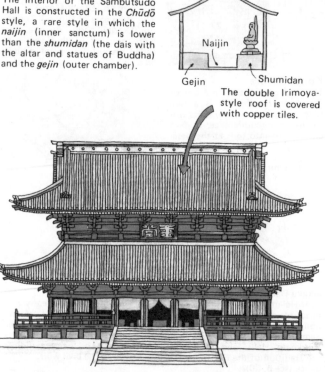

Naijin

Gejin

Shumidan

The double Irimoya-style roof is covered with copper tiles.

The three Buddha statues kept in the Sambutsu-dō Hall are considered to be transubstantiations of the three gods of Mt. Nikko, and as such are an extremely rare example of the fusion of *Shintō* and Buddhism. (See p. 15)

### Batō-Kannon (Horse-head Kannon)

This *Kannon\** with its horse's head (*Batō*) is believed to eat the trials and tribulations of mankind the way a horse eats grass. Its angry expression serves to admonish people for greed and laziness.

### Amida Nyorai

*Amida Nyorai*, one of the highest Buddhas, is believed to be the savior of mankind. Some sects teach that the way to get to the Buddhist heaven after death is to chant the phrase "*Namu-Amida-Butsu*" with single-minded devotion.

### Senju-Kannon

Another of mankind's saviors, the *Senju Kannon* is a Buddha with 1002 arms and 1002 eyes. Most statues of *Senju Kannon* are carved with only 4 arms, with the rear 40 each considered to have the power of 25.

The three Buddha statues are sculpted from *katsura* (Japanese Judas-tree) wood in the *Yosegi* style, in which separate pieces are carved and later joined together. They are lacquered and finished in gold leaf.

## Sōrin-Tō

The Sōrin-Tō is the topmost spire of a Gojū-no-tō (five-storied pagoda) without the rest of the pagoda, and is a representation of the tower originally used to house the remains of Buddha. The Sōrin-Tō at Rinnō-ji Temple contains 1000 holy scriptures and is 13.3 m high.

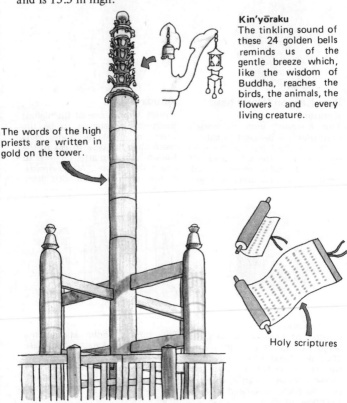

### Kin'yōraku

The tinkling sound of these 24 golden bells reminds us of the gentle breeze which, like the wisdom of Buddha, reaches the birds, the animals, the flowers and every living creature.

The words of the high priests are written in gold on the tower.

Holy scriptures

### Itowappu Tōrō

The two 6-m-tall bronze lanterns near the Sōrin-Tō were donated to the temple by the *Itowappu* Group, which had received sole trading rights from the Edo Shogunate to import raw silk, the most valued imported commodity of the time.

*Kasa* — hat

*Ho-bukuro* — lantern

*Ukedai* — seat for lantern

*Sao* — trunk

*Hasu* — Indian lotus flower

*Jirin* — skirt

*Kidan* — pedestal

Most of the prayers are for passing an exam, for a safe childbirth, or for health and prosperity.

### Gankaké-ema

An *ema* is a small wooden votive tablet, usually with a picture of a horse on the front, and a plea or prayer written on the back. The *ema* is hung up at a shrine or temple as a substitute for donating a real horse, and in the belief that the prayer will be answered.

The *ema* of Rinnō-ji Temple also have pictures of the twelve animals of the *jūnishi*, the Chinese zodiac. It is considered most effective to write one's prayer on an *ema* with a picture of the animal which represents the year of one's birth (see p. 40).

## Shōyō Garden

The Shōyō garden of Rinnō-ji Temple is a go-round style garden with paths winding around a long central lake, with Mt. Nantai and Mt. Nyohō in the background. The garden displays a different kind of beauty with each different season, and is considered a masterpiece of Edo-Era landscaping.

**Tō-tōrō (pagoda-style lantern)**
Lanterns in the form of pagodas became fashionable at the beginning of the Edo Era.

One of the arts of Japanese landscape gardening is to use the natural landscapes surrounding the garden for effect. This is known as *shakkei*, or "landscape borrowing".

This bridge is made from a single block of stone.

Japanese landscape gardening is a unique style of gardening which attempts to express all the beauty and wildness of nature in a limited space. The three main styles are the *Tsukiyama*, *Karé-sansui* and *Chaniwa* styles; the *Kaiyū* style, or go-round style, is a grand combination of all three.

Shinden hall

Tsukiyama / Island

The flow of water is represented by white sand.

Island

Ocean

## The Tsukiyama style

The term *Tsukiyama* refers to the process of piling up earth to represent mountains. Nature is depicted in a concrete way in this style of garden, with a lake representing the sea, and hedges representing forests. The island usually constructed in the center of the lake represents *Shinsen* Island, an island inhabited by the *sennin*, or holy men, of Chinese legend.

## The Karé-sansui style

This abstract style of garden uses only rocks and white sand to depict nature. The sand represents seas and rivers, and the rocks represent mountains, islands, boats, dragons, etc. This type of garden is strongly influenced by *Zen**, and is used by *Zen* priests as an object of contemplation during their meditations.

## The Chaniwa style

Developed along with *chadō**, the Way of Tea, this style of garden attempts to express the uniquely Japanese concept of *wabi*, which eschews gaudiness and extravagance and seeks true beauty in commonplace, timeworn objects such as *ishi-dōrō* (stone lanterns) and *tobi-ishi* (stepping-stones).

Tobi-ishi stones

Ishi-dōrō (stone lantern)

Tsukubai (stone basin)

# GŌHAN-SHIKI

In this strange ceremony, held at the Sambutsu-dō Hall of Rinnō-ji Temple on April 2, the participants are forced to eat large quantities of boiled rice. This ceremony is said to derive from the custom of Nikko's *yamabushi* (mountain priests) of offering food to Buddha, and is said to bring happiness and avert misfortune.

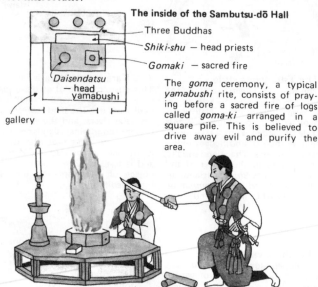

**The inside of the Sambutsu-dō Hall**

Three Buddhas

*Shiki-shu* — head priests

*Gomaki* — sacred fire

*Daisendatsu* — head yamabushi

gallery

The *goma* ceremony, a typical *yamabushi* rite, consists of praying before a sacred fire of logs called *goma-ki* arranged in a square pile. This is believed to drive away evil and purify the area.

## Saito Ō-goma-ku

In this ceremony, held prior to the *gōhan-shiki* ceremony, a priest dressed as a *yamabushi* and carrying a holy sword prays in front of the sacred fire known as *goma*.

### Kinkō

This horned straw headband, called *kinkō*, is a sign that the wearer has been chosen as the recipient of divine favor.

### Gōhan-Chōdainin

The *gōhan-chōdainin*, those who play the role of being forced by the *yamabushi* priests to eat 3 *shō* (1.5 gallons) of rice, are thought to earn themselves a year of good fortune by their part in the ceremony. In former times, there was great competition among generals and local barons to be chosen for the role. Now, the participants are chosen by lottery from the congregation of Rinnō-ji Temple.

**Gōhan-chōdainin**

The rice is accompanied by dishes of *tadé* (smartweed), *tōgarashi* (red pepper), *daikon* (Japanese radish) and other Nikko delicacies.

The *gōhan-chōdainin* sit holding the bowls of rice, and *yamabushi* priests called *gōhan-sō* stand in front of them crying "Korya! Korya!" and flourishing large *kiseru* (long-stemmed tobacco pipes) and sticks called *udegoro*. The ceremony is brought to a close by the priests flinging their sticks and pipes to the floor. The *gōhan-chōdainin* do not actually have to eat the rice.

◆延年の舞

# ENNEN-NO-MAI

This traditional dance is performed every year on 17 May in the Sambutsu-dō Hall of Rinnō-ji Temple. The performance lasts for only 15 minutes. The dance, said to have been brought to Nikko by the priest Jikaku Daishi, who learnt it in China, is performed alternately by two priests wearing white helmet-like headcloths called *Gojō-gesa*, who dance facing the three Buddha statues in the hall. The dance is performed in prayer for national peace.

*Katō* — white cowl

*Hitataré* — red cloth

*Ōguchi-bakama* — white divided skirt

The *Ennen-no-Mai* is danced powerfully with the arms outstretched, moving in a straight line. An interesting feature is that the movements do not match the rhythm of the holy invocations chanted in the background.

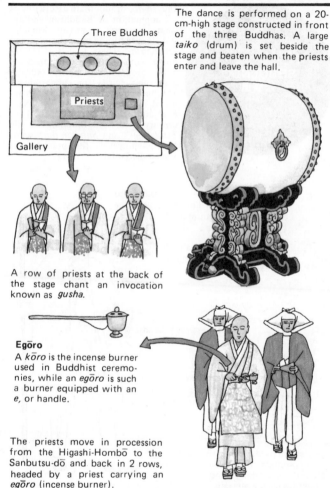

Three Buddhas

Priests

Gallery

The dance is performed on a 20-cm-high stage constructed in front of the three Buddhas. A large *taiko* (drum) is set beside the stage and beaten when the priests enter and leave the hall.

A row of priests at the back of the stage chant an invocation known as *gusha*.

**Egōro**
A *kōro* is the incense burner used in Buddhist ceremonies, while an *egōro* is such a burner equipped with an *e*, or handle.

The priests move in procession from the Higashi-Hombō to the Sanbutsu-dō and back in 2 rows, headed by a priest carrying an *egōro* (incense burner).

**SHUGENDŌ**
修験道

*Shugen-dō,* or mountain asceticism, is a combination of Buddhism and ancient Japanese mountain worship, and is practiced by priests called *yama-bushi.* These priests strive through worship and ascetic practices in the mountains to purify and prepare their spirits for enlightenment. This branch of Buddhism was established in the early part of the Nara Era\* and became popular in the 14th century with the founding of the *Tendai-shū\** and *Shingon-shū\** sects. Now, however, the practice has almost died out.

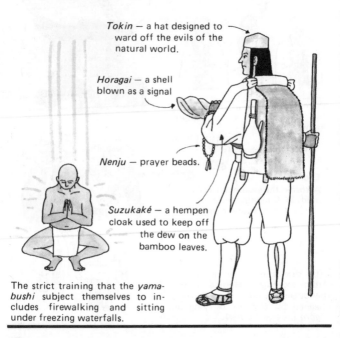

*Tokin* — a hat designed to ward off the evils of the natural world.

*Horagai* — a shell blown as a signal

*Nenju* — prayer beads.

*Suzukaké* — a hempen cloak used to keep off the dew on the bamboo leaves.

The strict training that the *yama-bushi* subject themselves to includes firewalking and sitting under freezing waterfalls.

# TŌSHŌGŪ SHRINE

To build Tōshōgū Shrine, the huge mausoleum erected to the memory of Tokugawa Ieyasu, the first *jhogun**of the Edo Era*, a total of 4,540,000 craftsmen and laborers are said to have worked for a period of twenty years. The shrine, completed in 1636, contains 500 kg of gold and 370 kg of silver, and construction costs amounted to the equivalent of $150,000,000. The shrine is a unique piece of religious architecture, combining both shrine architecture and Buddhist temple architecture, and is said to house the spirits of Buddha, the *Shintō** gods, and the deified spirit of Tokugawa Ieyasu himself. From the Yōmei Gate, one of the finest wooden constructions in the Orient, to the smallest of the buildings inside the shrine compound, all are carved, gilded, and decorated with rich colors. The beautiful paintings and elaborate furnishings inside the buildings are reminders of the luxurious tastes of the early Edo Era, the period when the *shōgun* were at the peak of their power and influence.

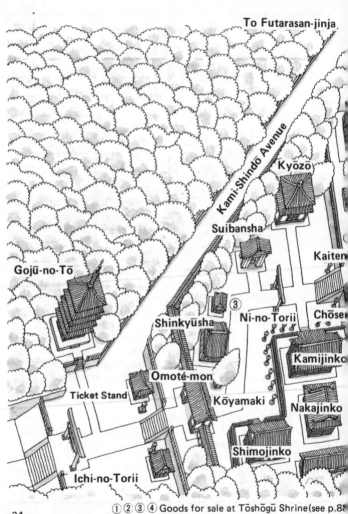

To Futarasan-jinja

Kami-Shindō Avenue

Kyōzō

Suibansha

Kaiten

Gojū-no-Tō

③

Shinkyūsha

Ni-no-Torii

Chōse

Kamijinko

Omoté-mon

Ticket Stand

Kōyamaki

Nakajinko

Shimojinko

Ichi-no-Torii

34

① ② ③ ④ Goods for sale at Tōshōgū Shrine (see p.88

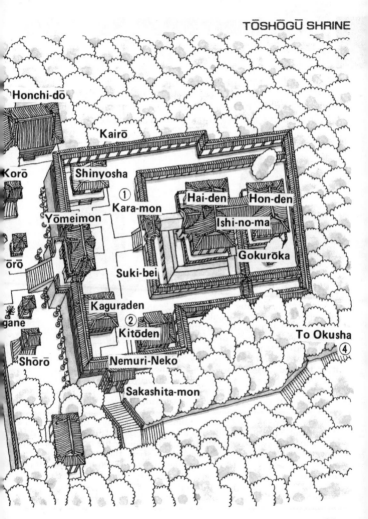

Honchi-dō

Kairō

Koro

Shinyosha

① Kara-mon

Yōmeimon

Hai-den

Hon-den

Ishi-no-ma

ōrō

Gokurōka

Suki-bei

Kaguraden

gane

② Kitōden

To Okusha

④

Shōrō

Nemuri-Neko

Sakashita-mon

◆徳川家康

# TOKUGAWA IEYASU

The chief deity of Tōshōgū Shrine, Tokugawa Ieyasu (1542 – 1616), was a brilliant general and politician who lived in the *Sengoku Jidai\** (Warring States Era), when Japan had no central government and was racked by wars between local barons.

**A portrait of Tokugawa Ieyasu at Tōshōgū Shrine**
Tokugawa Ieyasu stated in his will that after his death he would become a god and watch over the fortunes of the House of Tokugawa, and that he should be enshrined at Mt. Nikkō one year after he had passed away. This was the signal for the start of the mammoth construction operation that produced Tōshōgū Shrine.

**Namban Dōgusoku**
The helmet and armor worn by Tokugawa Ieyasu were imported from the West and reworked in Japan.

Tokugawa Ieyasu's will also contained his philosophy of life. In it, he stated that "life is like carrying a heavy burden; it is best not to rush ahead too hastily. He who accepts it as natural for life not to go exactly how he wants it to will not feel dissatisfied. Rather than doing too much, it is best to leave some things undone. When managing others, give full rein to their good points and overlook their weak points". Many of his sayings on managing people are still followed by Japanese businessmen today.

Through his many military victories and astute political tactics, he eventually succeeded in uniting and bringing peace to the country. The Edo Shogunate, the government that he established at Edo (present-day Tokyo) wielded absolute power and lasted for more than 260 years, an unrivaled period of stability in Japan's history. Besides its religious function, Tōshōgū Shrine also served as a symbol of the Edo Shogunate's domination.

### The Battle of Sekigahara

This battle, the biggest in the history of Japan, was fought in 1600 between the rival armies of the Toyotomi Family and Tokugawa Ieyasu. With his victory in this battle, Tokugawa Ieyasu became *shōgun*, the supreme ruler of Japan.

The *Sengoku Jidai* (Warring States Era) produced the three military geniuses Oda Nobunaga, Toyotomi Hideyoshi* and Tokugawa Ieyasu. The characters of these three men are exemplified by the metaphor of the nightingale which would not sing. In such a situation, Oda Nobunaga would kill the bird as useless, and Toyotomi Hideyoshi would make every effort to get it to sing; but Tokugawa Ieyasu would wait patiently until it started to sing by itself. In the event, Tokugawa Ieyasu became the outstanding figure of the three.

# ICHI-NO-TORII

A *torii* is the gate which marks the entrance to a *Shintō* shrine and reminds visitors that they are about to enter holy ground. The Ichi-no-Torii, or first *torii*, of Tōshōgū Shrine located at the end of the Omoté-Sandō (the avenue leading up to the shrine), is the largest stone *torii* in Japan. It is 9m tall and its pillars are 3.6m in girth. The grounds of Tōshōgū Shrine begin at this gate.

**Kasa-ishi**
The *kasa-ishi* (transom, or capstone) of the Ichi-no-Torii is in three pieces for better absorption of vibration.

**Shimenawa**
The *shimenawa,* a holy rope used to keep out evil spirits, is found at all *Shintō* shrines.

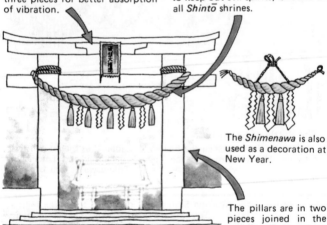

The *Shimenawa* is also used as a decoration at New Year.

The pillars are in two pieces joined in the middle, allowing them to absorb shock better.

The Japanese archipelago has many active volcanoes and is one of the most earthquake-prone areas of the world. Great care was taken in the construction of Tōshōgū Shrine to protect it from the effects of earth tremors.

38

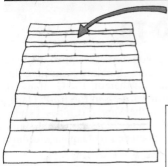

The ten stone steps leading into the shrine from the Ichi-no-Torii become gradually narrower and shallower. This trick of perspective makes the steps appear to extend farther into the distance than they actually do.

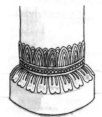

### Ni-no-Torii

The Ni-no-Torii, or second *torii*, was the first bronze *torii* in Japan. The *torii* is the symbol of a *Shintō* shrine, but this particular one has pedestals in the shape of *hasu*, or lotus flowers, the symbol of Buddhism. The gate thus symbolizes the coexistence of Buddha and the gods of *Shintō*. (See p.14)

### Terifuri-Ishi

The stone in the center of the second step form the top, called *Terifuri-Ishi,* changes color with the weather. The right-hand side of this stone is brown and the left blue, and the contrast between the two colors strengthens on humid or rainy days.

### The origin of the Torii

The word *torii* is written with the Chinese characters for "bird" and "dwelling", and was originally the roosting-place of the chickens to be sacrificed at the shrine. Most *torii* are made of wood and are painted red.

◆五重の塔

# GOJŪ-NO-TŌ

The Gojū-no-Tō, or five-storied pagoda, was developed in China from the Indian stupa, a round domed building enshrining the remains of Buddha, or representations thereof. The Gojū-no-Tō at Tōshōgū Shrine, with its four lower tiers in the *Wayō* (Japanese) style and its topmost tier in the *Karayō* (Chinese) style, was purposely decorated in rich, vibrant colors to make it stand out against the background of dark-green *sugi* (Japanese cedars).

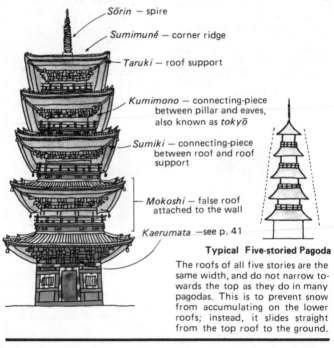

*Sōrin* — spire

*Sumimuné* — corner ridge

*Taruki* — roof support

*Kumimono* — connecting-piece between pillar and eaves, also known as *tokyō*

*Sumiki* — connecting-piece between roof and roof support

*Mokoshi* — false roof attached to the wall

*Kaerumata* —see p. 41

**Typical Five-storied Pagoda**

The roofs of all five stories are the same width, and do not narrow towards the top as they do in many pagodas. This is to prevent snow from accumulating on the lower roofs; instead, it slides straight from the top roof to the ground.

The twelve animals of the Chinese *jūni-shi* (the Oriental Zodiac) are carved on the *kaerumata* of the first storey.

*Kaerumata* ("frog-crotch") is a slang term for the *tokyō*, the assembly that supports the roof. The term derives from the *tokyō*'s shape.

The *jūni-shi*, the Oriental equivalent of the Western Zodiac, uses twelve animals to represent the points of the compass, the date, and the time.

| Ne | Ushi | Tora | U | Tatsu | Mi |
|------|--------|------|------|------|------|
| 1948 | 1949 | 1950 | 1951 | 1952 | 1953 |
| 1960 | 1961 | 1962 | 1963 | 1964 | 1965 |
| 1972 | 1973 | 1974 | 1975 | 1976 | 1977 |
| Uma | Hitsuji | Saru | Tori | Inu | I |
| 1954 | 1955 | 1956 | 1957 | 1958 | 1959 |
| 1966 | 1967 | 1968 | 1969 | 1970 | 1971 |
| 1978 | 1979 | 1980 | 1981 | 1982 | 1983 |

Those who believe in the *jūni-shi* believe that a person's fate is strongly influenced by his or her birth-sign, or *eto*. Since the *jūni-shi* operates on a 12-year cycle, the ages 12, 24, 36, 48, etc. are especially important, and people of these ages are considered particularly likely to meet with great good or bad fortune.

◆表門

# OMOTÉ-MON

The Omoté-mon, or Front Gate, also known as Niō-mon, is guarded by two *koma-inu* (shrine dogs) and two *Niō* (Devas) and boasts 66 other carvings, both large and small. This richly-decorated eight-legged gate also symbolizes the coexistence of *Shintō* and Buddhism, since *Niō* statues are usually used in Buddhist temples and *koma-inu* in *Shintō* shrines

**Kara-jishi with botan (peonies)**
The *kara-jishi*, or Chinese lion, is a typical subject in Japanese painting and sculpture. Since the lion is not a Japanese animal, most of these representations are highly imaginative adaptations of deer, wild boar and other indigenous beasts.

**Baku**
The *baku* is a mythical Chinese animal which eats people's dreams.

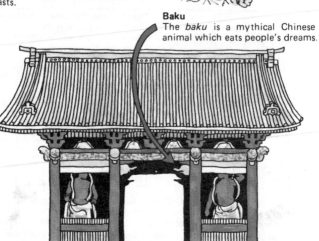

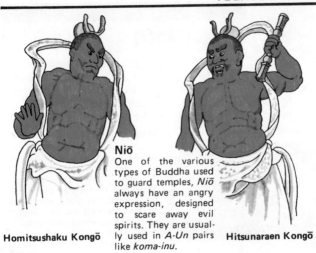

**Homitsushaku Kongō**

### Niō
One of the various types of Buddha used to guard temples, *Niō* always have an angry expression, designed to scare away evil spirits. They are usually used in *A-Un* pairs like *koma-inu*.

**Hitsunaraen Kongō**

*"Un"* symbolizes death.

*"A"* symbolizes life.

### Koma-inu
*Koma-inu* are the holy dogs invariably found guarding the entrances of shrines. The one on the right always has its mouth open and is called *A*, while its partner on the left has its mouth closed and is called *Un*. Together they represent the process of inspiration and exhalation, and the phrase *"a-un-no-kokyū"* or *"a-un* breathing"* means a state of communication so intimate that thoughts are transmitted instantly, without the need for words.

◆三神庫

# SAN-JINKO

The three red buildings to the right of the Omoté-mon are known as San-Jinko. They consist of a lower (Shimo-Jinko), a middle (Naka-Jinko) and an upper (Kami-Jinko) building, and are used to house the costumes and equipment worn by the 1200 people who take part in the *Sennin Musha Gyōretsu* parade (see p. 82).

(see p. 82)

### Imaginary Elephants

This carving, on the side *(tsuma)* of the Kami-Jinko, is one of the three most important carvings at Tōshōgū Shrine. The carving is based on a painting by the famous artist Kanō Tan'yū*, who is said to have painted the two animals after reading about elephants in a book, even though he had never actually seen any of the beasts.

Hira

Kōhai

Tsuma

### Kami-Jinko

Constructed with a roof in the *Kiritsuma*\* style, this building includes a *kōhai,* or place of prayer. The front of the building, facing the Sandō (the main avenue in the shrine precincts), is called *tsuma,* and the sides are called *hira.*

44

### Kōhai

Visitors to a shrine stand and say their prayers on the landing at the top of the steps in front of the main entrance. This area, usually protected from the weather by extended eaves, is called *kōhai*.

## Naka-Jinko

This building has an *Irimoya*-style* roof and three *kōhai*.

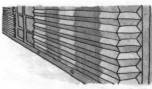

**The Azekura Architectural Style**
All three of the San-Jinko are constructed in the *Azekura* architectural style, with floors raised off the ground in the style known as *Takayuka-shiki*. The *Azekura* style employs triangular-sectioned cross-beams in the construction of the walls. These beams expand on wet and rainy days, sealing the walls tightly, and dry out and shrink on hot days, leaving gaps. This has the effect of maintaining the temperature inside the building steady.

## Shimo Jinko

This building has a roof in the *Kiritsuma** style and features three doors, even though there is only one room inside.

◆水盤舎

# SUIBAN-SHA

The Suiban-sha is the place where visitors to the shrine wash their hands and rinse their mouths as an act of purification before praying. The roof, with its *kara-hafu\**, or decorative gable, is adorned with carvings related to water and is supported by twelve granite pillars.

**Nami-ni-Hiryū**
A green dragon flying through the storm, kicking out at the mountainous waves that threaten to engulf it.

**Mizu-ni-Koi**
This *koi*, or carp, is colored black and ultramarine, and is coated in gold leaf.

This *Suiban* was a gift to the shrine from a Kyūshū *daimyō* (local lord) in 1618.

## Purifying oneself at the chōzu-ya

*Chōzu-ya* is the more usual name of the *suiban-sha,* the place where visitors to a shrine purify themselves before praying. The water used for this is known as *chōzu.* It should be treated with respect and should not be drunk greedily.

1. Take some water in the *hishaku* (ladle) in the right hand and pour it over the left.

2. Switch the ladle to the left hand and pour water over the right.

4. Pour water over the right hand once more, and wipe hands and lips with a clean handkerchief.

3. Rinse the mouth with water held in the cupped right hand. Do not bring the ladle to the mouth.

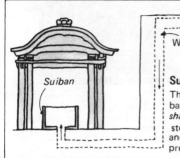

Water pipe

### Suiban

The *suiban* is the large granite basin under the roof of the *suiban-sha.* The water flows down the stone wall behind the *suiban-sha* and wells up into the basin under pressure.

◆神厩舎

# SHINKYŪ-SHA

The Shinkyū-sha is the stable where the sacred horses used in ceremonies at the shrine are kept. The left-hand side of the roof is extended in the *Nagaré\** style, and there are five carvings featuring monkeys on the front and three at the side.

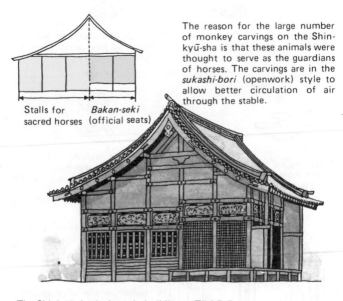

Stalls for sacred horses

*Bakan-seki* (official seats)

The reason for the large number of monkey carvings on the Shinkyū-sha is that these animals were thought to serve as the guardians of horses. The carvings are in the *sukashi-bori* (openwork) style to allow better circulation of air through the stable.

The Shinkyū-sha is the only building at Tōshōgū Shrine in the *Shiraki* style, which uses plain instead of painted wood. It contrasts strongly with the other shrine buildings, all of which are richly colored.

The eight monkey carvings represent the way of life held to be ideal by the people of the time, which was to avoid unreasonable ambition, shun quarrels and strife, respect and care for one's parents, and create a happy and peaceful family life.

Parents should love their children and hold their future happiness at heart.

Children should hear, see and speak no evil, learning only that which is good.

Adults should consider their situation carefully and come to an independent judgement about their own future.

No matter how high a position one achieves, there is always a higher. Since ambition has no limits, it should be kept within reasonable bounds.

Friends should help and console each other in failure. Failure should not be feared, since "every cloud has a silver lining".

Everyone should find themselves a suitable mate and plan their way of life together.

Together, a couple can overcome all of life's problems.

When a couple eventually have children and raise a family is when they really appreciate their blessings and their obligation to their parents.

◆本地堂

# HONJI-DŌ

The Honji-dō hall houses a statue of *Yakushi-Nyorai*, the Buddhist Physician of Souls, and is the largest building at Tōshōgū Shrine. Its exterior is a typical example of *Shintō* architecture, with its *Irimoya*-style* roof and *kōhai* (place of prayer), but the interior is in the pure Buddhist-temple architectural style.

### Nakiryū (the Roaring Dragon)

If one stands under the head of the large black dragon painted on the ceiling of the Honji-dō and claps one's hands loudly, a shriek said to resemble the cry of the dragon can be heard.

### Juni-jinshō

These twelve gods are the guardians of Yakushi-Nyorai, the Buddhist Physician of Souls. Each corresponds to a different month on the *jūni-shi,* the Chinese calendar, and many people regard the god corresponding to the month in which they were born as their own personal guardian deity.

# The Lanterns of Tōshōgū

There are 121 *tōrō* (lanterns) in the precincts of Tōshōgū Shrine, all of which are lit at special ceremonies and events. Most of these were donated to the shrine and are arranged with those given by people of highest rank nearest the center of the grounds.

### Oranda Tōrō
This octagonal-roofed lantern contains thirty candle-stands.

### Hasu Tōrō
This lantern, constructed in the shape of a candelabrum, has 31 candle-holders and is notable for its Western design.

### Kaiten Tōrō
This nine-sided copper lantern was imported from Holland in 1634. It is 4-m-tall and rotates about its vertical axis. The *aoi* (hollyhock) crests on the top, the crest of the *Tokugawa-ké\** (the House of Tokugawa) are upside-down.

### Namban Tetsu Tōrō
The only iron lantern at Tōshōgū Shrine, this was imported from Portugal. The word *namban,* or "Southern barbarian", was used to refer to Western countries in general.

# SHŌRŌ/KORŌ

A *shōrō*, or belfry, is a place where a shrine or temple bell is hung, while a *korō* is where a *taiko*, or big drum, is placed. Tōshōgū festivals always used to start with the sound of the *taiko* and finished with the sound of bells The *shōrō* and *korō* at Tōshōgu Shrine are no longer used, however, and their doors are always kept closed.

**Katō-mado**
This type of window, unique to Buddhist temple architecture, is in the shape of a flame. This is the origin of its name, which literally means "fire-head window".

**Kōran**
This balustrade is painted red in the Chinese style.

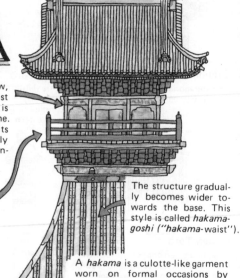

The structure gradually becomes wider towards the base. This style is called *hakama-goshi* ("*hakama*-waist").

A *hakama* is a culotte-like garment worn on formal occasions by nobles and *bushi (samurai)* *. Nowadays, it is worn only at Japanese-style weddings and other traditional ceremonies.

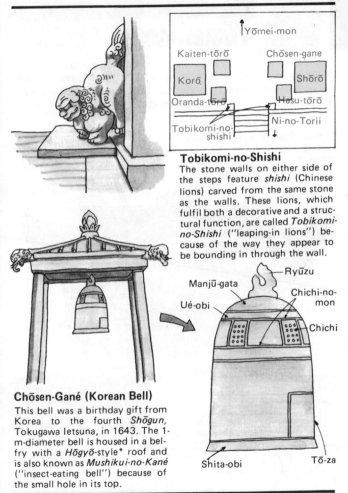

## Tobikomi-no-Shishi

The stone walls on either side of the steps feature *shishi* (Chinese lions) carved from the same stone as the walls. These lions, which fulfil both a decorative and a structural function, are called *Tobikomi-no-Shishi* ("leaping-in lions") because of the way they appear to be bounding in through the wall.

## Chōsen-Gané (Korean Bell)

This bell was a birthday gift from Korea to the fourth *Shōgun*, Tokugawa Ietsuna, in 1643. The 1-m-diameter bell is housed in a belfry with a *Hōgyō*-style* roof and is also known as *Mushikui-no-Kané* ("insect-eating bell") because of the small hole in its top.

◆陽明門

# YŌMEI-MON

The Yōmei-mon, or Yōmei Gate, the most important building at Tōshōgū Shrine, was built by 130,000 craftsmen working on an unlimited budget. In the Edo Era*, ordinary people were not permitted to pass through this gate, and even the Emperor's

A fish with a humorous face, known as *gegyo,* can be seen above the *kara-hafu* * at the front of the gate.

This plaque bears Tokugawa Ieyasu's alias, *Tōshō Daigongen.*

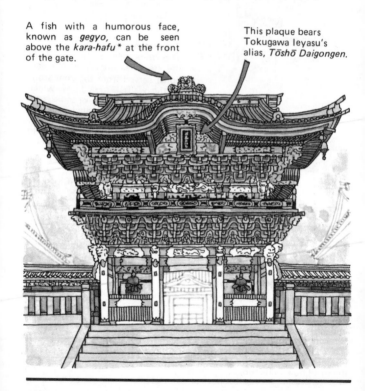

envoy had to change into formal dress before being allowed to enter. The richness of its color, based on black, white and gold, and the beauty and intricacy of its carvings, of which there are more than four hundred, provide an unrivaled feast for the eyes. The gate is also called *Higurashi-mon,* or Sunset Gate, since it was felt quite possible to gaze on the gate from dawn to sunset, so enraptured by its beauty that one would completely forget the passage of time.

## Kairō

The carvings on the galleries to the left and right of the Yōmei Gate represent air (clouds), earth (flowers, birds and animals) and water (waterfowl) in order from top to bottom.

## Zuijin

*Zuijin* were originally officers responsible for guarding the members of the Imperial family, but later became deified as the guardians of the shrine. Their costume is the formal costume of the Heian Era*.

## Nobori-Ryū Happō-Nirami

The name *Nobori-Ryū* means a dragon *(ryū)* climbing *(nobori)* straight towards Heaven. The *Nobori-Ryū* painted in black on the ceiling inside the Yōmei Gate is called *Happō-Nirami* ("staring in all directions") because it appears to be looking at the viewer from whatever direction it is viewed.

Around the gate are 22 carvings representing the life of the *Sennin* (hermits, or holy men) of ancient China. Most of these designs were derived from old Chinese folk tales and legends.

*Dankin* (playing the *koto*, or Japanese harp).

*Igo* (playing the game of *go\**)

*Sojin Sannin* (petitioning the Emperor of China)

*Shūkō Chōso* (Shūkō, one of the Emperors of China, listening to the petition).

*Kōshi Kanga* (Confucius gazing upon a river, absorbed in thought)

*Tensho* (reading a book)

*Kanga* (looking at a picture)

A carving depicting *Karako* (Chinese children) at play.

## Menuki-no-Ryū

This huge dragon is carved from a single tree-trunk. It appears to be flying through the air, quite separate from the gate.

## Ryūma

This imaginary creature has the head of a dragon and the legs of a horse.

The carvings on the side of the gate feature brightly-colored peonies that stand out vividly from their gold background.

## Mokumé-no-Tora

This carving of a tiger makes full use of the natural grain of the *keyaki* (zelkova) wood from which it is carved.

## Saka-Bashira

The pattern on one of the pillars at the back of the gate is upside-down. This deliberate mistake was introduced to mar the perfect beauty of the gate lest it should attract devils or misfortune.

## EDO-ERA CULTURE
## 江戸時代の文化

In the period of great political stability that was the Edo Era, art and culture gradually lost its previous boldness and extravagance and became more refined and detailed. The cultural center of Japan moved from the location of the Emperor's court in *Kamigata* (Kyoto and Osaka) to that of the *shōgun*, at Edo (Tokyo), and the emphasis switched from architectural works and sculpture to paintings and handicrafts.

The best-known *ukiyoé* artists are Katsushika Hokusai, for his landscapes; Sharaku, for his *yakushaé* (pictures of *kabuki* artists); and Utamaro, for his *bijinga* (portraits of women).

### Ukiyoé
*Ukiyoé,* or woodblock prints, were developed in the Edo Era. Most of them depict contemporary scenes, landscapes, famous beauties, or *kabuki* actors, and most of those remaining today are the colored ones known as *nishikié.*

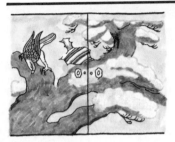

## Kanō Tan'yū

One of the most famous painters of the Edo Era, Kanō Tan'yū was renowned for the splendor and magnificence of his masterpieces, many of which can be seen at Tōshōgū Shrine. His most famous work is the "Pine Tree with Hawk" at Kyoto's Nijō Castle.

## Mikaeri Bijin

This famous *ukiyoé* is the work of the founder of the genre, Hishikawa Moronobu. Postage stamps featuring this *ukiyoé* are among the most expensive of Japanese stamps.

## Kabuki

*Kabuki,* one of Japan's best-known stage arts, was popular among the common people during the Edo Era. It was at first performed only by young girls, but the authorities prohibited this as corrupt, and the roles were taken over by men, thus establishing the style which has continued to the present day. *Kabuki* actors were as popular as modern stars of stage and screen, and their *ukiyoé* portraits were the equivalent of the publicity photographs of today.

◆神輿舎

# SHIN'YO-SHA

The Shin'yo-Sha is the building which houses the three *mikoshi* (portable shrines) used in Tōshōgū Shrine's spring and autumn *taisai* (grand festivals). Each of these huge *mikoshi* weighs 750 kg and is carried by 75 men. They are dedicated to the fame and fortune of the House of Tokugawa, and there is one each for the three *shōgun* Tokugawa Ieyasu, Toyotomi Hideyoshi, and Minamoto-no-Yoritomo.

A *tennyo* dancing with flowers.

A *tennyo* playing the *fué* (flute).

A *tennyo* playing the *biwa* (Japanese lute).

### Tennyo Sōgaku-zu

The circular centerpiece of the *kagami-tenjō* (mirror ceiling) inside the Shinyo-sha is covered in gold leaf and depicts the beautiful celestial nymphs known as *tennyo* playing musical instruments and dancing joyfully.

60

**Minamoto-no-Yoritomo (1147-1199)**

The first of Japan's *shōgun*, Minamoto-no-Yoritomo rose from the strife of the latter part of the Heian Era* to establish a military government. This started the period of control of Japan by the military which was to last to the end of the Edo Era, a period of more than 700 years.

**Toyotomi Hideyoshi (1536-1598)**

A military genius who succeeded in reuniting Japan after the *Sengoku Jidai** (Warring States Era). He undertook two military expeditions to Korea in the hope of conquering China, but failed, and died of an illness the year after his last expedition. The House of Toyotomi was then broken up by Tokugawa Ieyasu and the foundations of the Edo Shogunate were laid.

**Tokugawa Ieyasu**

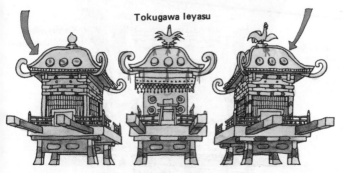

A *mikoshi* is a portable shrine into which the gods of the main shrine are believed to descend at festivals. The *mikoshi* is carried energetically around the locality to drive away evil spirits and bring good fortune to the area.

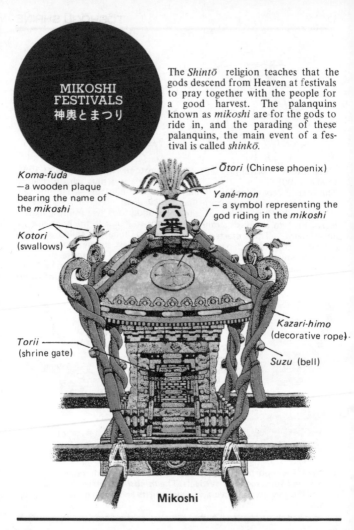

## MIKOSHI FESTIVALS
## 神輿とまつり

The *Shintō* religion teaches that the gods descend from Heaven at festivals to pray together with the people for a good harvest. The palanquins known as *mikoshi* are for the gods to ride in, and the parading of these palanquins, the main event of a festival is called *shinkō*.

*Koma-fuda*
—a wooden plaque bearing the name of the *mikoshi*

*Kotori* (swallows)

*Torii* (shrine gate)

*Ōtori* (Chinese phoenix)

*Yané-mon* — a symbol representing the god riding in the *mikoshi*

*Kazari-himo* (decorative rope)

*Suzu* (bell)

**Mikoshi**

A *mikoshi* with the paper decorations called *shinai*.

A *mikoshi* with burning firewood, called *kaen-mikoshi*.

A *futon-mikoshi*, with *futon* bedding on the roof.

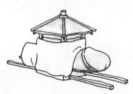

A *mikoshi* in the shape of a penis.

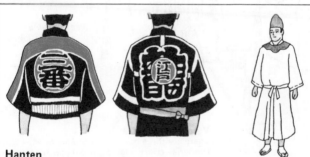

## Hanten

*Mikoshi* are usually carried by groups of men and women wearing *hanten,* the short-sleeved jackets worn by Edo-Era firemen. The *hanten* carry a *daimon,* the crest of the local town association, on the back. At Nikko's festivals, however, the *mikoshi* are carried by people wearing the costumes of *shinshoku* (*Shintō* priests).

63

◆神楽殿

# KAGURA-DEN

*Kagura*, sacred *Shinto* music and dance, came into existence in the 9th century and is now performed at shrines all over Japan. The Kagura-den (*Kagura* Hall) at Tōshōgū Shrine consists of a stage (*butai*) and a backstage room called *Shōzoku-no-ma*, and is used at festivals for performances of *kagura* by *miko* (shrine maidens) known as *ya-otomé*.

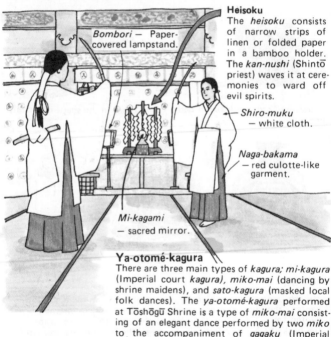

**Bombori** — Paper-covered lampstand.

**Heisoku**
The *heisoku* consists of narrow strips of linen or folded paper in a bamboo holder. The *kan-nushi* (Shintō priest) waves it at ceremonies to ward off evil spirits.

*Shiro-muku* — white cloth.

*Naga-bakama* — red culotte-like garment.

*Mi-kagami* — sacred mirror.

**Ya-otomé-kagura**
There are three main types of *kagura*; *mi-kagura* (Imperial court *kagura*), *miko-mai* (dancing by shrine maidens), and *sato-kagura* (masked local folk dances). The *ya-otomé-kagura* performed at Tōshōgū Shrine is a type of *miko-mai* consisting of an elegant dance performed by two *miko* to the accompaniment of *gagaku* (Imperial court music).

*San-karado* — a Chinese-style folding door which opens in the center.

The Kagura-den is designed to allow performances to be viewed from outside.

*Shitomi-do* — The top half of this latticework window can be pulled up to let in light and air.

**A gagaku performance**

*Shō* (Bamboo wind instrument)

*Yokobué* (bamboo flute)

*Biwa* (4-stringed lute)

*Koto* (13-stringed harp)

*Kakko* (small drum)

*Shōko* (metal percussion instrument)

*Taiko* (large drum)

## Gagaku

*Gagaku,* the music used in *kagura* performances, is a development of the Chinese court music introduced into Japan in the 7th century. It has a stately rhythm and beautiful melodies, and is performed on a combination of percussion, wind and string instruments.

65

◆唐門

# KARA-MON

The Kara-mon (Chinese Gate) is the gate leading to the Honden and other main buildings of Tōshōgū Shrine. In the Edo Era*, only those of sufficiently high rank to meet the *shōgun* himself were allowed to pass through this gate. The main buildings are enclosed by a beautiful windowed wall *(sukibei)* with the Kara-mon in its center.

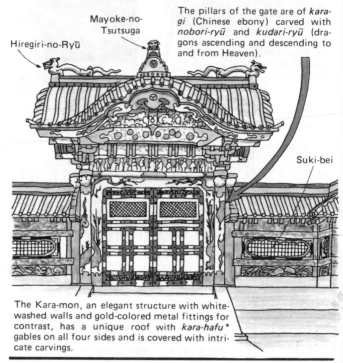

Mayoke-no-Tsutsuga

Hiregiri-no-Ryū

The pillars of the gate are of *kara-gi* (Chinese ebony) carved with *nobori-ryū* and *kudari-ryū* (dragons ascending and descending to and from Heaven).

Suki-bei

The Kara-mon, an elegant structure with white-washed walls and gold-colored metal fittings for contrast, has a unique roof with *kara-hafu*\* gables on all four sides and is covered with intricate carvings.

This carving of Chinese holy men was made from a single tree and depicts 26 of the sages in 3 rows. The carving is designed so that all of the faces can be seen when it is viewed from the front.

### Hiregiri-no-Ryū ("Dragons with clipped wings")

The dragons on the east and west ends of the roof guard the gate during daylight. Since they appear so lifelike, their wings and tails are clipped to prevent them flying away.

### Mayoké-no-Tsutsuga

The *tsutsuga* is a mythical Chinese beast said to be even stronger than dragons or *shishi* (Chinese lions). The *tsutsuga* on the front and back of the roof of the Kara-mon guard the gate at night. Their forelegs are fastened with metal rings to stop them getting away.

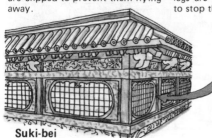

The latticework is decorated with flower patterns.

### Suki-bei

This 160-m-long wall features gold-latticed windows with green frames topped by beautiful carvings designed to be viewed from a variety of angles.

◆拝殿

# HAI-DEN

The *hai-den*, the hall of worship in front of the *hon-den*, or main sanctuary, of a shrine, is where prayer services are held. The Hai-den at Tōshōgū Shrine is split into three halls, the left for the Imperial family, the right for the *shōgun*, and the central hall for conducting services. All the carvings and paintings in the Hai-den are masterpieces by the most celebrated artists of the time.

**Gō-tenjō (coffer ceiling)**
100 different dragons in a circular design decorate the sunken panels of the coffer ceiling.

**Sanjūrokkasen**
These portraits are of the 36 most famous poets of the Heian Era*.

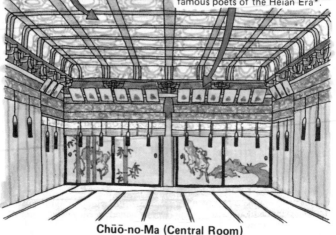

**Chūō-no-Ma (Central Room)**

### Kirin (Chinese unicorn)

This *kirin*, painted by the famous artist Kanō Tan'yū in rich colors on a gold background, guards the hall during the day.

### Baku

The night-time guardian of the hall is the dream-eating *baku*, also painted by Kanō Tan'yū.

### Hōō

This mythical Chinese bird, thought to appear whenever a king is to be born, resembles a *kirin* in front and a deer behind, and has a snake's head, a fish's tail, a turtle's back, a swallow's chin, and a chicken's beak. This picture is in the Imperial family's hall.

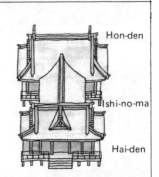

The Hai-den and the Hon-den are connected in an H pattern by the Ishi-no-Ma (the Stone Room). This style of layout is called *Gongen*.

◆石ノ間

# ISHI-NO-MA

Most shrines have a separate *hon-den* and *hai-den*, but at Tōshōgū Shrine, these two buildings are connected by a corridor known as the Ishi-no-Ma. This 5.5 m-wide, 9.6 m-long chamber is ornately decorated, with the gold of the paintings and carvings becoming richer as the Hon-den is approached.

### Kintaka-Makié

This 1.8 m-high, 1 m-wide *tsuma-do* (double door) is decorated with a plum tree on the right and a tree peony on the left, worked in *taka-makié* (raised gold lacquer).

A pair of richly-colored *koma-inu** (see p.43) guard the entrance to the Honden.

The name of the corridor, Ishi-no-Ma (the Stone Room) derives from the flagstones that form its floor.

◆本殿

# HON-DEN

The Hon-den is dedicated to the spirit of the guardian deity of Tōshōgū Shrine, Tokugawa Ieyasu. The holiest building in the shrine, it consists of a *hei-den* (offertory room), a *nai-jin* (inner sanctuary), and a *nai-nai-jin* (innermost sanctuary), where Tokugawa's spirit is believed to dwell.

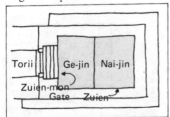

**The interior of a typical shrine's hon-den**

The *nai-nai-jin* contains a sacred area called *Gokū-den,* where the spirit of Tokugawa Ieyasu, flanked by those of Toyotomi Hideyoshi* on the left and Minamoto-no-Yoritomo* on the right, is enshrined' What the *nai-nai-jin* contains is a closely-guarded secret, known only to a few select members of the shrine hierarchy.

The interior of the Hon-den is decorated with works by the most famous artists of the time, using the finest materials available.

A brightly-colored *shishi* (Chinese lion) on a gold background, by Kanō Tan'yū.

A *ryōmen-bori* (double-sided carving) of the heavenly maidens known as *tennyo.*

# GOKU-RŌKA/NEMURI-NEKO

The Goku-Rōka, the corridor connecting the Ishi-no-Ma with the long gallery that has the Yōmei-mon at its center, is used for carrying offerings to the Hon-den. One of the three most important carvings at Tōshōgū Shrine, the *Nemuri-Neko*, or Sleeping Cat, is on a *kaerumata\** in this corridor near the Saka-shita-mon Gate.

### Goku-Rōka

The *hō-ō* (Chinese phoenix) and other carvings on the *tobi-kōryō* (the lateral beams forming the upper part of the corridor) are particularly beautiful.

### Nemuri-Neko

This masterpiece by the famous Edo-Era\* architect-cum-sculptor Hidari Jingorō gave rise to various theories about its significance, since cats had rarely been used to decorate shrines until that time. Some of these theories are:

1) It signifies that nothing impure or contaminated, not even a single mouse, is allowed to pass this point.

2) It poses the *Zen-mondō*, or catechetical question, "which is more appealing, the peonies or the sleeping cat?" The correct answer to this is said to be "It's nothing to do with me".

3) The cat sleeping in the warm sunshine among the peonies represents sunlight, *nikkō* in Japanese.

◆坂下門

# SAKASHITA-MON

This gate was used by the *shōgun* when they visited Tōshōgū Shrine to pray. The gold fittings stand out richly against the whitewashed pillars and carvings. This is one of the few original structures built in 1617.

The ceiling is decorated with carvings of *botan* (peonies), *kiku* (chrysanthemums) and other flowers.

The upper beams are carved with pine trees and cranes, symbols of good luck and prosperity.

The doors are carved in a *karakusa*\* pattern featuring *botan* (peonies).

◆奥社

# OKUSHA

The Okusha, at the back of the shrine compound, consists of a gate called the Inuki-mon, a pagoda called Hōtō, and a hai-den, or hall of worship. The remains of Tokugawa Ieyasu are kept in the Hōtō.

### Hōtō

The Hōtō is a small bronze pagoda mounted on an octagonal stepped stone dais. The reason for its simplicity, even though it holds the remains of Tokugawa Ieyasu, is that the Japanese do not generally believe that a person's soul stays in his or her remains after death.

The story is told that when Shaka (Buddha) was living the life of a missionary, a pagoda sprung up suddenly from the ground in front of him. The pagoda's doors opened and the figure of Nyorai, one of the highest buddhas, emerged. This was the first *Hōtō*, or sacred pagoda.

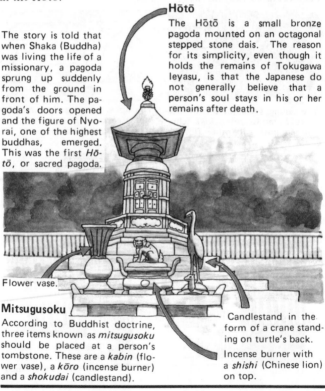

Flower vase.

Candlestand in the form of a crane standing on turtle's back.

Incense burner with a *shishi* (Chinese lion) on top.

### Mitsugusoku

According to Buddhist doctrine, three items known as *mitsugusoku* should be placed at a person's tombstone. These are a *kabin* (flower vase), a *kōro* (incense burner) and a *shokudai* (candlestand).

### Hai-den

The hall of worship for visitors to the Okusha, the hai-den is in the *Shintō* style, while the pagoda is Buddhist. This matter-of-fact combination of *Shintō* and Buddhism is one of the unique characteristics of Tōshōgū Shrine.

All the metal fittings on the black-lacquered hai-den are engraved in minute detail in the style known as *ke-bori*, or hairline engraving.

The 207 stone steps leading up to the Okusha from the Sakashita-mon are all single blocks of stone, and the wall on either side of the gate is also made from hollowed-out blocks.

### Kanō Sugi

This old *sugi* (Japanese cedar) beside the hon-den is protected by a *shimé-nawa,* or sacred rope. It is said that if one faces the hole in its trunk and prays, one's prayers will be answered. The bark is full of coins stuck there by people wishing for good luck.

# SHRINE ARCHITECTURE
神社建築

Japan's indigenous religion, Shinto-ism, is a form of animism or shamanism which deifies seas, mountains, plants, animals and all things in nature. *Shintō* shrines, built to house various *shintai*, or sacred objects, are built in a style which shows some Chinese influence but is essentially Japanese.

## The Nagaré Style
This style of shrine has a *Kiritsuma*-style roof with one side extended to cover the prayer area.

## The Kasuga Style
This has a *Kiritsuma*-style roof with a penthouse built into the front. The prayer area is under this penthouse.

## The Irimoya Style
This style features a roof which slopes down on all four sides from a central peak. It is one of the most important styles of shrine architecture along with the *Nagaré* and *Kasuga* styles.

## The Gongen Style
In this style, of which Tōshōgū Shrine is one of the best-known examples, the *honden* and *haiden* are linked by a corridor to form an H pattern.

## The typical layout of a Shintō Shrine

The buildings in the precincts of a Shintō shrine are laid out in a more or less standard pattern regardless of the scale of the shrine. The entrance is marked by a *torii*, from which a *sandō*, the avenue used by visitors to the shrine, leads to the *Hai-dan* and *Hon-den*. The *shintai* are kept in the *Hon-den*, but the ordinary congregation is not allowed inside this building and can only go as far as the *Hai-den* to say their prayers.

---
## Roofs
---

Roofs are constructed in a variety of styles and are covered with materials such as tiles, copper sheet, bark, thatch and wooden boards.

**The Kiritsuma Style**
This is the most orthodox type of roof style, with two sloping sides divided lengthwise by a central ridge.

**The Yosemuné Style**
A rectangular roof with four sloping sides.

**Hafu** — A decorative gable.

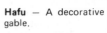

*Kara-hafu*

**The Irimoya Style**
A combination of the *Kiritsuma* and *Yosemuné* styles.

**The Hōgyō Style**
A square roof decorated at the peak with a metal ball called *hōju*.

*Chidori-hafu*

## BUDDHIST TEMPLES
## 仏教寺院

Buddhism was introduced into Japan from China in the 6th century, and the construction of Buddhist temples began in earnest with its adoption as the state religion. Buddhist temple architecture can be divided into two main styles, *Wayō* (Japanese style) and *Karayō* (Chinese style), but many of the different sects developed their own individual styles of construction.

### Wayō

The *Wayō* style, originally introduced from China in the 7th century, was refined and developed until it became uniquely Japanese.

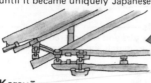

### Karayō

The *Karayō* style, similar to that prevalent in 12th-century China, was introduced into Japan along with *Zen\** and is also known as the *Zenshū* style.

### Tokyō

Traditional Japanese architecture dispenses with nails or other metal parts, so various complex joints and fittings are needed to hold the structure together. The *tokyō,* or *kaerumata,* the assembly connecting the roof to the pillars, is regarded as the most important part of a building's structure and identifies the style of the building.

## Buddhist Statues

The form of Buddhism prevalent in Japan is *Daijō-Bukkyō* (Mahayana Buddhism), in which it is believed that numerous Buddhas join forces with Siddhartha, the founder of Buddhism, in the work of saving the world. These lesser Buddhas and the statues and images representing them can be divided into four main types; *Nyorai, Myō-ō, Ten* and *Bosatsu.*

### Bosatsu

*Bosatsu,* or Bodhisattva, help people find their way to the Buddhist heaven. The female *Bosatsu* called *Kannon* rank with *Nyorai* as the most important gods in the Buddhist hierarchy.

### Nyorai

*Nyorai,* or Tathagata, symbolize truth and are also believed to be holy representations of Siddhartha.

### Myō-ō

*Myō-ō,* the servants or altered forms of *Nyorai,* act as destroyers of evil spirits and guardians of the Buddhist faith.

### Ten

Called Deva, or Giver of Light, in Sanskrit, *Ten* control the various worlds inhabited by humans, such as the physical world and the world of desire.

# SENNIN MUSHA GYŌRETSU

The *Sennin Musha Gyōretsu* (Procession of a Thousand Warriors) is a huge parade of people dressed in the military garb of the Edo Era\*. It takes place on the day after Tōshōgū Shrine's *Reitaisai* (Grand Spring Festival), held on May 17, and re-enacts the procession which bore the remains of Tokugawa Ieyasu from Sumpu (the old name for what is now Shizuoka Prefecture) to their new resting-place at Nikko. It is also held on the day after the October 17 *Taisai* (Autumn Festival), but with only half the number of participants.

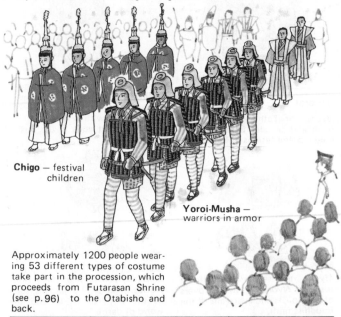

**Chigo** — festival children

**Yoroi-Musha** — warriors in armor

Approximately 1200 people wearing 53 different types of costume take part in the procession, which proceeds from Futarasan Shrine (see p. 96) to the Otabisho and back.

## Kakemen

This group is wearing the masks of foxes, the chubby-faced *Okamé*\* red devils, blue devils and other supernatural creatures. They represent a legend in which the ghosts, goblins and demons of Mt. Nikko gathered to pay their respects to Tokugawa Ieyasu.

The *mikoshi* housing the spirit of Tokugawa Ieyasu is brought to Futarasan Shrine on the day before the parade, and spends the night there. The Otabisho, or traveler's resting-place, is where the *mikoshi* is placed while its bearers take a well-earned rest.

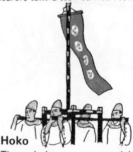

## Sarutahiko-no-Mikoto

The procession is led by Saruta-hiko-no-Mikoto, one of the long-nosed, red-faced goblins known as *Tengu*, who live deep in the mountains and possess supernatural powers such as the ability to fly and make themselves invisible.

## Hoko

Three *hoko*, or ceremonial halberds, appear at the head of the procession, one called *Hōken* (the Sacred Sword), one called *Nichirin* (the Mirror of the Sun) and one called *Getsurin* (the Mirror of the Moon).

81

## Shishi-Odori

The *Shishi-Odori*, or Lion Dance, is designed to frighten away evil spirits. Since Japan has never had wild lions, the costumes used in the dance resemble native animals such as deer and wild boar. The dance is common in farming areas throughout Japan and used to be regarded as a way of scaring off wild animals that might otherwise damage the crops.

## Shimba

The sacred horses stabled in the Shinkyu-Sha (see p.48) are called *shimba*. These horses are used in the parade to carry various *shintai* (sacred objects).

*Makura-gi* — platform on which the *mikoshi* is rested.

## Mikoshi

At festivals, the gods of the shrine are thought to descend from Heaven and enter the three *mikoshi*, which are normally kept in the Shin'yo-Sha (see p.60) but are brought out specially for the festivals and parades. The spectators throw offerings of money at the *mikoshi*, and children who have volunteered for this duty collect the money and take it to the shrine.

A *kannushi (Shintō* priest) in official vestments riding alongside the *mikoshi.*

*Yaotomé (miko,* or shrine maidens, who perform *kagura)* wearing white headcloths called *shirobōshi.*

## Ceremonies at the Otabisho

Various ceremonies are performed when the *mikoshi* arrive at the Otabisho, the half-way mark of the procession and the resting-place for the gods in their *mikoshi.*

### Hōhei Gyōji
In this ceremony, 75 types of food are offered to the gods. Since it is forbidden to walk along the corridor carrying a tray, the *shinkan* (priests) pass the food from hand to hand to the *hai-den* (hall of worship).

### Azuma-Asobi-no-Mai
*Azuma-Asobi* is a type of *kagura* performed to entertain the gods while they take their rest. Four dancers in red and white robes dance gracefully to the elegant rhythm of *gagaku\*.*

◆ 流鏑馬

# YABUSAMÉ

In this ceremony, originally a form of training for *bushi (samurai\*)*, mounted archers shoot their arrows at targets while riding at speed. The ceremony takes place at the Spring Grand Festival on May 17 at the special riding ground in Shimo-Shindō avenue. Before the event, mounted *samurai* and archers in the costume of the Kamakura Era parade, together with 80 young children, from in front of Nikko Station in the direction of Tōshōgū Shrine.

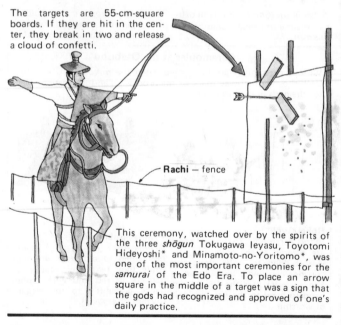

The targets are 55-cm-square boards. If they are hit in the center, they break in two and release a cloud of confetti.

**Rachi** — fence

This ceremony, watched over by the spirits of the three *shōgun* Tokugawa Ieyasu, Toyotomi Hideyoshi\* and Minamoto-no-Yoritomo\*, was one of the most important ceremonies for the *samurai* of the Edo Era. To place an arrow square in the middle of a target was a sign that the gods had recognized and approved of one's daily practice.

*Ayai-gasa* — straw hat

*Suikan* — silk underwear

*I-koté* — arm-brace

trousers

*Mukabaki* — leather overskirt

## Kari-Shōzoku

The costume worn for *Yabusamé*, called *Karishōzoku*, was the costume worn by *samurai* for hunting.

## Yumiya Watashi-shiki

In this ceremony, the archers taking part in the *Yabusamé* event receive purified bows and arrows from the Tōshōgū Shrine priests.

The cloth is not passed directly from hand to hand, but is presented and received using special rods.

## Nikkisho

The *nikkisho* is the place where the official who records the scores sits. When the event is over, the archer with the best score receives a white cloth as a mark of divine favor. To win this cloth was one of the highest honors that an Edo-Era\* *samurai* could aspire to.

# THE SHŌGUN OF THE EDO ERA
## 江戸時代の将軍

The Edo Era began in 1603, when Tokugawa Ieyasu (see p.36) became *shōgun* and established his *bakufu* (military government) in Edo (present-day Tokyo). Thus began a period of political stability which lasted for 264 years, until 1867, when the Meiji Restoration removed political control of Japan from the 15th *shōgun*, Tokugawa Yoshinobu, and restored it to the Emperor. Since Japan was virtually closed to the outside world during this period, it developed a unique and distinctive national unity and culture.

The *aoi* (hollyhock) crest, the symbol of the House of Tokugawa.

**Tokugawa Iemitsu**
The 3rd *shōgun*, Tokugawa Iemitsu (see p. 112), played a major part in laying the foundations of the Edo Shogunate.

## Sankin Kōtai
In one of his best-known political stratagems, Tokugawa Iemitsu forced the wives and children of the *daimyō* (local barons) to live in the capital, Edo, as hostages against the barons' good behavior. The barons were obliged to make a ceremonial visit to Edo every other year with a retinue of at least 100 followers, in a journey of between one and three months each way which cost an enormous amount of money and left them with no funds with which to plot insurrection. These visits were called *daimyō-gyōretsu,* and the system was known as *sankin-kōtai.*

Tsunayoshi's signet

## Tokugawa Yoshimuné
The 8th *shōgun*, Tokugawa Yoshi-muné, was known as an able leader who introduced numerous political reforms, including a law called *ken'yakurei* which prohibited extravagance, in an attempt to abolish corruption in government.

## Tokugawa Tsunayoshi
Feared as a tyrant, the 5th *shōgun*, Tokugawa Tsunayoshi, was extremely protective of animals and went so far as to pass a law which made it a capital offence to kill a dog.

*Shaguma* — yak hair dyed red

*Hachimaki* — headband

*Sansai-haori* — special haori, or half-coat

## Tokugawa Yoshinobu
The 15th and last *shōgun* of the Edo Shogunate, Tokugawa Yoshinobu assumed his title in 1866 and was forced to hand over power to the Emperor in 1867, one year later. This brought to an end the seven centuries' dominance of the *samurai* over Japan.

## The Meiji Restoration
As well as being a battle between the forces of the *shōgun* and those of the Emperor, the Meiji Restoration (*Meiji Ishin*) was also a struggle between those who supported *sakoku*, the closure of Japan to the outside world, and those who opposed it. This struggle, sparked off by the arrival of the American Navy in Japan, was won by opponents of *sakoku*, and Japan was thus launched on its way to becoming a modern state.

# Goods for Sale at Tōshōgū

Various sacred objects, lucky charms, etc., are on sale at almost all *Shintō* shrines. Strictly speaking, these items are not being sold, but are being given to visitors in exchange for a donation to the shrine. People display them in their homes or carry them around in purse or wallet in the hope of gaining good fortune.

### ① Omiki and Heishi

*Omiki* is sacred *saké* donated to a shrine. Drinking it is said to give health and longevity. It is served in a container called *heishi,* from which it is poured into flat dishes called *sakazuki* for drinking. *Heishi* and *sakazuki* are also on sale at shrines.

### ② Omikuji

*Omikuji* are fortunes printed on small slips of paper drawn at random. They usually contain information such as whether one can expect good or bad luck in business and other aspects of life, whether one's wishes will be granted, whether lost property will be recovered, how a love affair will turn out, etc. Many people use these as a guide to planning for the future. *Omikuji* written in English are available at some shrines, including Tōshōgū Shrine.

See the symbols ① - ④ on the map on pages 34 and 35 for where to buy these goods at Tōshōgū Shrine.

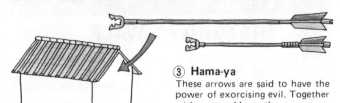

### ③ Hama-ya

These arrows are said to have the power of exorcising evil. Together with a sacred bow, they are sometimes left under the rafters when a new house is built to protect it from misfortune.

### ④ Kano Suzu

Buying one of these bells, which commemorate a visit to the Oku-sha, or Inner Shrine, is believed to ensure that one's wishes will come true.

### ④ Nemuri-Neko Ema

This special kind of *ema,* made from Nikko cedar, carries a picture of the famous Sleeping Cat (*Nemuri-Neko,* see p. 72).

### Shichi-go-san

*Shichi-go-san,* held on Nov. 15, is a festival at which people pray that their children will grow up happy and healthy. Three-year old girls, five-year-old boys, and seven-year-old girls are dressed in their best clothes (*haregi,* either colorful *kimono* or Western dress) and taken to shrines to pray.

89

# HISTORICAL WALK

Nikkō is fortunate in having many beautiful sights, both man-made (Tōshōgū Shrine, Rinnō-ji Temple, etc.) and natural (Lake Chūzenji, Kegon Falls, etc.). But besides these major

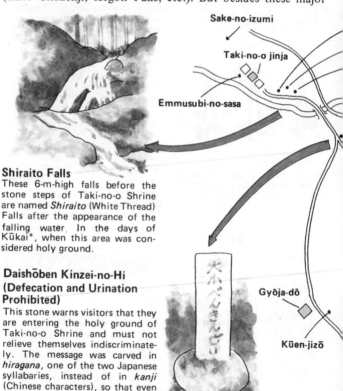

Sake-no-izumi

Taki-no-o jinja

Emmusubi-no-sasa

Gyōja-dō

Kūen-jizō

## Shiraito Falls

These 6-m-high falls before the stone steps of Taki-no-o Shrine are named *Shiraito* (White Thread) Falls after the appearance of the falling water. In the days of Kūkai\*, when this area was considered holy ground.

## Daishōben Kinzei-no-Hi (Defecation and Urination Prohibited)

This stone warns visitors that they are entering the holy ground of Taki-no-o Shrine and must not relieve themselves indiscriminately. The message was carved in *hiragana*, one of the two Japanese syllabaries, instead of in *kanji* (Chinese characters), so that even semi-literate people could read it.

attractions, there are also large numbers of historical relics, rich in mystery and legend. Some of these can be seen along the 3.2-km stone-paved path which runs through the cedar woods from Shinkyō (see p. 16) to Taki-no-o Shrine. To walk this path, whose name, *Shiseki Tanshō*, literally means "path for exploring historic relics", is to set back the clock and take a trip through ancient history and legend.

Undameshi-no-torii

Yōbō-seki

Bessho-ato

Iimori-sugi

Shimmé-no-Hi

Tegaké-ishi

Kaizan-dō

Hotoke-iwa

Kannon-dō
(Kyōsha-dō )

Onyō-seki

Tōshōgū

### Kitano-Jinja Shrine

Although called a shrine, Kitano Shrine has no buildings and consists only of a small stone *hon-den* and a few large rocks. It is dedicated to Sugawara Michizané*, the god of learning, and it is believed that praying here will bring success to one's academic studies and improve one's handwriting.

### Hotoké-iwa (Buddha stones)

The six *ten*, the guardians of the Buddhist faith, are carved in the hollows of the rocks behind the Kaizan-dō Hall.

◆滝尾神社

# TAKI-NO-O SHRINE

This shrine was built in 820 by Kūkai* and dedicated to the goddess of Mt. Nyohō, Tagori-Himé-no-Mikoto. Because of its long history, the traditions observed in its ceremonies and festivals form the basis of many of Nikko's religious events. As well as the Rō-mon (Tower Gate), hai-den (worship hall) and hon-den (main hall), there are many historic relics to be found at the shrine.

The stone around the hole has been worn down by the many pebbles that have struck it.

### Un-dameshi-no-Torii

The stone *torii* in front of the Rō-mon has a round hole in its upper part. It is believed that anyone who can throw three stones in succession through this hole while making a wish will have their wish granted.

### Hon-den

The red-painted hon-den has a roof in the *Nagaré* style. There are doors in the back which open to allow worshippers to pray to Mt. Nyohō.

**Kūkai (774 – 835)**
This Heian-Era* priest went to China in 804 to study Buddhism and returned to Japan in 806 to found the Shingon-shū* sect. He was also known as an accomplished poet and a master of calligraphy.

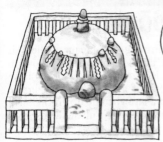

## Emmusubi-no-Sasa

These sacred bamboos stand in the grounds of the shrine. It is said that anyone who holds two of the leaves together, one from each bamboo, with the thumb and little finger of each hand, will be able to marry their true love.

## Kodané-Ishi ("Child-Seed Stone")

Many people wanting children visit this 1-m-high round rock to pray, since it is said to have the miraculous property of bestowing fertility on those who desire it.

*Saisen-bako* — offertory box

*Saké*, or rice wine, is made from rice, *kōji* (malted rice which acts as a yeast), and water.

**Tokkuri**

**Masu**

**Choko**

## Saké-no-Izumi

The water from the Saké-no-Izumi, a 2-m-diameter spring surrounded by a wooden fence, is said to taste like *saké*. This water is revered by *saké* makers, since it is reputed to make excellent *saké*.

## How to drink saké

*Saké* can be drunk hot, as *atsukan*, by heating it in a *tokkuri* (flask) and drinking it from the small cups called *choko*; or cold, as *hiya-zaké*, from glasses or the small wooden boxes called *masu*.

◆香車堂

# KYŌSHA-DŌ HALL

*Kyōsha,* one of the pieces used in *shōgi,* or Japanese chess, is similar to the castle in Western chess and can only move in straight lines. This attribute has led to the use of special large *kyōsha* as an offering in the hope of a safe birth, i.e., in the hope that the baby will move in a straight line down the birth canal. The offerings of *kyōsha* are collected in the Kyōsha-dō Hall, which is often visited by expectant mothers.

Before the baby is born, the mother borrows a *kyōsha* from the hall, and if the baby is born safely, she returns the original *kyōsha* plus one extra. Recently, some mothers have taken to donating an *ōshō* (king) in the hope that their child will grow up strong.

### Shōgi

*Shōgi* resembles Western chess in that the winner is the first to checkmate his or her opponent's king. However, it is far more complex than chess, since the opponent's captured pieces can be used as one's own.

◆興雲律院

# KŌUNRITSU-IN TEMPLE

Kōunritsu-in Temple, built in 1729, belongs to the *Tendai-shū* sect. The main hall enshrines a gilded wooden statue of *Amida Nyorai*, flanked by two *Kannon*. Praying at this temple has long been believed effective in curing sickness and ensuring the birth of healthy babies.

*Kara-hafu* *

*Katō-mado* window

### Shōrō-mon Gate
A shōrō-mon is a gate with a *shōrō,* or belfry, mounted on the top. The gate at Kōunritsu-in Temple has curved white walls and unusual *katō-mado* windows.

### Ritsu-in Etsunen-sai
This New Year's festival is held at Kōunritsu-in Temple every year on January 14, the last day of the solemn rituals which used to be held for the two weeks beginning on 1 January. In the festival, bad luck is driven away by setting up a *Fudō-son* Buddha in the temple grounds and performing ceremonies such as lighting a holy *goma** fire called *Otakiagé* and scattering lucky beans.

Beans are scattered to drive out bad luck and bring in good. This ceremony is usually performed at the *Setsubun* festival on February 3. Those scattering the beans cry *"Oni wa soto, fuku wa uchi"* ("Devils out, happiness in")

95

◆二荒山神社

# FUTARASAN SHRINE

Mt. Futara, also known as Mt. Nantai (see p.138), stands to the west of Nikko, and has been believed since ancient times

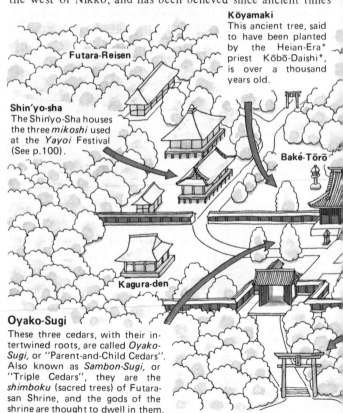

**Kōyamaki**
This ancient tree, said to have been planted by the Heian-Era* priest Kōbō-Daishi*, is over a thousand years old.

**Futara-Reisen**

**Shin'yo-sha**
The Shin'yo-Sha houses the three *mikoshi* used at the *Yayoi* Festival (See p.100).

**Baké-Tōrō**

**Kagura-den**

**Oyako-Sugi**
These three cedars, with their intertwined roots, are called *Oyako-Sugi,* or "Parent-and-Child Cedars". Also known as *Sambon-Sugi,* or "Triple Cedars", they are the *shimboku* (sacred trees) of Futara-san Shrine, and the gods of the shrine are thought to dwell in them.

to be the gathering-place of the gods of the mountains. The Futarasan Shrine complex, built by Shōdō Shōnin (see p.14), and dedicated to these gods, consists of the Hon-sha, or main shrine, on the slopes of Mt. Nikko, the Chūgūshi on the shore of Lake Chūzenji, and the Okumiya at the peak of Mt. Nikko.

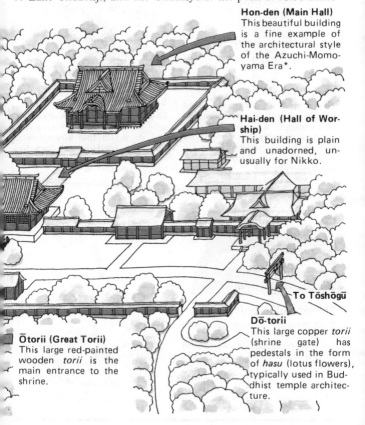

**Hon-den (Main Hall)**
This beautiful building is a fine example of the architectural style of the Azuchi-Momoyama Era*.

**Hai-den (Hall of Worship)**
This building is plain and unadorned, unusually for Nikko.

**To Tōshōgū**

**Dō-torii**
This large copper *torii* (shrine gate) has pedestals in the form of *hasu* (lotus flowers), typically used in Buddhist temple architecture.

**Ōtorii (Great Torii)**
This large red-painted wooden *torii* is the main entrance to the shrine.

## Bake-Tōrō

This copper lantern, made in the Kamakura Era*, is said to change into a demon when lit. There are ten sword-marks on it made by *samurai* guards attempting to kill it. It is lit only once a year, at the *Yayoi* Festival.

## Emmusubi-no-Sasa

The god of love is believed to reside in this *sasa* (bamboo grass), and it is said that anyone who opens an *omikuji* and then ties it on the plant will be able to marry their true love.

## Shichifukujin Omikuji

Each *omikuji* (a paper slip with one's fortune written on it) contains an *o-mamori* (lucky charm) of the *Shichifukujin* (the seven Chinese gods of good fortune) on it. Anyone wishing to become rich should put this in their purse or wallet and keep it with them at all times.

## Kenshu (offerings of saké)

The clear water of Mt. Futarasan makes excellent *saké,* and the *saké* makers who use this water donate barrels of their *saké* as offerings to the shrine.

At some traditional Japanese weddings, the bride and groom break open a cask of *saké* with a wooden mallet. This ceremony, known as *kagami-wari,* is the equivalent of the cake-cutting ceremony at Western weddings. It is also performed at other celebratory occasions.

*Saké* from the cask is called *taru-zaké.* It is best drunk from the small wooden boxes known as *masu,* with a pinch of salt on the corner.

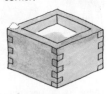

## Futara Reisen

There are various legends about the supposed miraculous properties of this spring, such as that it sometimes changes into *saké,* or that drinking it improves one's IQ. Visitors can drink *ocha* (green tea) or *amazaké* (a sweet, milky-colored, slightly-alcoholic rice beverage) made with the spring water at the thatched *azuma-ya,* or tea arbor, nearby.

◆弥生まつり

# YAYOI MATSURI

*Yayoi Matsuri* (The *Yayoi* Festival), the 1200-year-old main festival of Futarasan Shrine, is held every year from April 13 to 17. Its name derives from the fact that *Yayoi* is the third month on the lunar calendar, April on the modern calendar. The main attraction of the festival is the gorgeously-decorated *yatai* (parade floats), which converge on the shrine from various points of Nikko city. The festival marks the arrival of spring in Nikko.

The *yatai* are guided by a leader who bangs together a pair of wooden blocks called *hyōshigi*. This custom is needed because a quarrel can start if two *yatai* collide, or if their cherry branches so much as touch.

There is a pecking-order for those pulling the *yatai*, with the more important people at the front and the lesser mortals bringing up the rear.

### Hana-Yatai

The festival floats used at the *Yayoi* Festival are called *Hana-Yatai* (Flower Floats) because of the cherry blossoms which adorn the front and back of their roofs.

100

The black-lacquered *Hon-yatai* (Main Float), the only one kept at the shrine itself, is the most elegantly decorated of all the *yatai* taking part in the festival.

The *yatai* groups refresh themselves with food and *saké* on their way back from the shrine. When dusk falls, they light the lanterns and pull the *yatai* back to the town.

Many of the children carry a *shakujō*, a metal staff decorated with two rings like that said to have been used by Shōdō Shōnin. (See p.14)

Beautifully-costumed children riding on the *yatai* play "Yayoi-Bayashi" festival music on *fué* (flutes), *taiko* (drums) and other instruments. They practice for over a year for this occasion.

*Hana-kanzashi* — ornamental hairpins in the form of flowers

*Shakujō* — staff

*Chōchin* — paper lantern

The gods of the three mountains Mt. Nantai, Mt. Nyohō and Mt. Tarō are believed to dwell in the Futarasan Shrine complex, with the father (Mt. Nantai) enshrined at the Hon-sha, or main shrine, the mother (Mt. Nyohō) at Takino-o Shrine (see p.98), and their son, Mt. Tarō, at Hongū Shrine (see p.18). On April 14, the three gods assemble at the Hon-sha and descend into the three *mikoshi* normally kept there, and the *mikoshi* with the gods of Mt. Nyohō and Mt. Tarō aboard are then taken to their respective shrines. On 16th, they are brought back to the Hon-sha, and *kagura* and various other ceremonies are held there on the 17th. Then, on the same day, the three *mikoshi* are paraded round Tōshōgū Shrine and Rinnō-ji Temple before being returned to the Hon-sha of Futarasan Shrine.

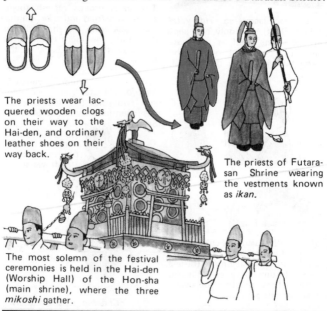

The priests wear lacquered wooden clogs on their way to the Hai-den, and ordinary leather shoes on their way back.

The priests of Futarasan Shrine wearing the vestments known as *ikan*.

The most solemn of the festival ceremonies is held in the Hai-den (Worship Hall) of the Hon-sha (main shrine), where the three *mikoshi* gather.

## Festival Stalls

At the *Yayoi* Festival, the main avenue leading to the shrine is lined with stalls of all kinds offering food, drink, toys and amusements, heightening the festival mood.

**Wata-amé**
This spun-sugar confection is the equivalent of Britain's candy floss or America's cotton candy.

**Tako-yaki**
These grilled wheat-flour dumplings contain small pieces of *tako* (octopus) and are eaten with a soy-based sauce.

These 3cm. dumplings contain small pieces of *tako* (octopus). 10 of them make one serving, and they are eaten with a toothpick after being seasoned with brown sauce.

**Kingyo-sukui**
In this game, goldfish are scooped from a shallow tank with paper-covered wire spoons. The trick is to put the spoon into the water at an angle and catch the goldfish with the metal part.

These stalls are also called *yo-misé* (night stalls) because of the colorful and lively atmosphere they create after dark. Many of their owners make a living by going from festival to festival all over the country.

# FESTIVAL FLOATS
## 屋台とまつり

In many Japanese festivals, the *mikoshi* are followed in the *shinkō* parade by antique floats known as *yatai*, first used in the 9th century at Kyoto's *Gion* Festival. The *yatai* are elaborately-decorated affairs made by the best craftsmen and artists of the area, and many of them carry orchestras composed of *chigo* (costumed and made-up children) performing the festival music known as *hayashi*.

**The Gion Festival** (1 — 29 July, Kyoto)
This huge festival, which lasts for most of July each year, is said to have been started in 869 in an effort to halt the spread of an epidemic which was sweeping Kyoto. It is one of Japan's most important and best-known festivals, and features 31 richly-decorated floats, with performances of the beautiful music known as *Gion-bayashi*.

**Hikiyama Matsuri** (13 – 16 April, Nagahama City, Shiga Pref.)
The special *Hikiyama* floats used at this festival have stages on which children perform *kabuki*.

**Hitachi Fūryūmono** (3–5 May, Hitachi City, Ibaraki Pref.)
These mammoth floats, which feature puppets performing plays known as *fūryūmono*, are 15-m-tall and are built in seven tiers.

**Nebuta** (2 – 7 August, Aomori City, Aomori Pref.)
The purpose of the *Nebuta* festival is to drive away the spirits of sleep and wash them down the rivers to the sea. It is known for its huge floats depicting *kabuki* actors and legendary heroes, and ranks with the *Gion* Festival and Osaka's *Tenjin* Festival as one of the three biggest in Japan.

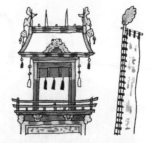

**Takayama Matsuri** (14 and 15 April, 9 and 10 Oct, Takayama City, Gifu Pref.)
The festival floats appearing at this festival are masterpieces of Japanese art and craft. From the puppets that decorate them down to the tiniest carved details, every item is an example of the pinnacle of Edo-Era art. So splendidly decorated are they that they are also known as "Yōmei Gates in Motion".

# FUTATSU-DŌ HALL

In front of the Ō-torii of Futarasan Shrine stand two halls, the Jōgyō-dō Hall and the Hokké-dō Hall. Because these two buildings are almost identical, they are also known as Futatsu-dō, or Twin Halls. Both were built in 848, and are *dōjō*, or schools, of Buddhist learning, the Jōgyō-dō Hall for the training known as *Jōgyō-zammai* and the Hokké-dō Hall for that known as *Hokké-zammai*.

The two halls are connected by a corridor, from the center of which a path leads to the Jigen-dō Hall.

**Jōgyō-dō Hall**

**Hokké-dō Hall**

Although the two buildings are very similar, the Jōgyō-dō Hall is in the Japanese style and the Hokké-dō Hall in the Chinese style, and they have different roof decorations *(hōju)* and windows. The main Buddhas enshrined in the halls are *Amida Nyorai* in the Jōgyō-dō Hall and *Shaka-Nyorai* in the Hokké-dō Hall.

◆慈眼堂

# JIGEN-DŌ HALL

Jigen-dō Hall was built in 1645 as the mausoleum of Jigen Daishi (see p.21). Besides its hai-den and granite pagoda, the hall is known for its rare documents collected by Jigen Daishi. These are kept in a *kyōzō*, or repository for Buddhist scriptures, called *Tenkai-zō*.

**The hai-den of Jigen-dō Hall**

**The tomb of Jigen Daishi**
This 3-m-tall, five-storied stone pagoda is guarded by 6 *Ten* (Buddhist guardian deities).

This stone in the shape of a roof was formerly the roof of the *suibansha*, the spring at which visitors to the temple purify themselves before entering.

**Tenkai-zō**
This old storehouse for documents was built in 1646.

# NIKKO CRAFTS

Since the Edo Era, when the best woodcarvers from all over Japan gathered at Nikko for the construction of Tōshōgū Shrine and imparted the secrets of their arts, Nikko has been famous for its craft products. Many visitors take some of these intricately-carved and decorated items home as souvenirs when they visit Nikko.

Each of the items in a *Nikko Cha-dōgu* set is made individually on a lathe.

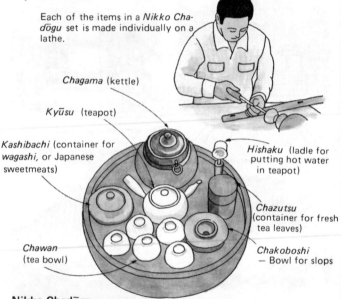

*Chagama* (kettle)

*Kyūsu* (teapot)

*Kashibachi* (container for *wagashi,* or Japanese sweetmeats)

*Hishaku* (ladle for putting hot water in teapot)

*Chazutsu* (container for fresh tea leaves)

*Chawan* (tea bowl)

*Chakoboshi* — Bowl for slops

### Nikko Chadōgu

This is a complete miniature set of the utensils used in *chadō,* the tea ceremony. Long recognised as a typical Nikko souvenir, the sets are notable for their detail and the way different woods and colorings are used for the different items.

## Nikko-bori

*Nikko-bori,* a style of wood-carving handed down from the Edo Era, is distinguished by its representations of plum, peony, chrysanthemum and other flowers, finished by staining lightly. Various items are available, from hand mirror to tables.

Plaques with *kamon* (family crests) carved on them are available at Nikko souvenir shops. Customers can have their name carved beside the *kamon* if they order it specially.

The tops are woven from bamboo bark.

## Nikko geta

These *geta* (clogs) are a combination of the usual *geta* and *zōri,* straw sandals, and are specially for use in snowy areas. Their supports are wide and stable and have good waterproof and insulating properties.

*Geta* are wooden clogs with two supports, while *zōri* are flat sandals woven from bamboo bark or straw. Both are fitted with thongs called *hanao* which fit between the big toe and the one next to it. *Geta* are formal, *zōri* informal.

# DAIYŪIN-BYŌ

Daiyūin-byō is the mausoleum of Tokugawa Iemitsu, the third shōgun, grandson of Tokugawa Ieyasu. It is less richly decorated and has fewer buildings than nearby Tōshōgū Shrine,

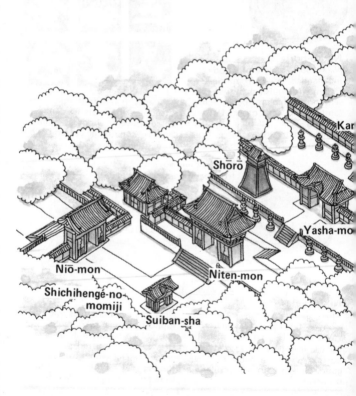

since Iemitsu left instructions in his will that his mausoleum should be less magnificent than that of Ieyasu, the grandfather whom he loved and respected. Construction was started in 1652 and finished with amazing speed only 14 months later. The structure provides an interesting contrast with Tōshōgū Shrine.

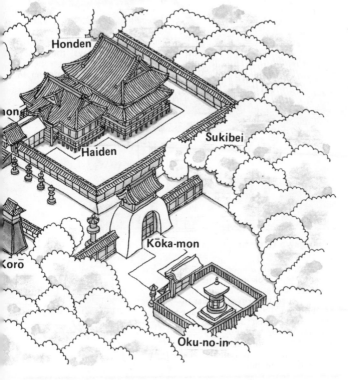

111

## Suiban-sha

The *suiban-sha*, the place where visitors to the shrine purify themselves by rinsing their mouth and hands, has a *Kiritsuma*-style* roof with a *kara-hafu** gable supported by twelve granite pillars. An interesting feature is that the pillars are inclined inwards at the top.

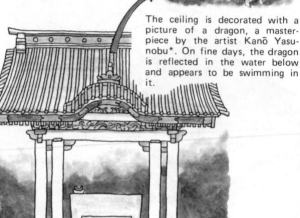

The ceiling is decorated with a picture of a dragon, a masterpiece by the artist Kanō Yasunobu*. On fine days, the dragon is reflected in the water below and appears to be swimming in it.

## Tokugawa Iemitsu (1604 – 1651)

The third *shōgun* of the Edo Shogunate, Tokugawa Iemitsu was a clever politician who strengthened his grip on power by establishing the *sankin-kōtai** system and closing Japan to the outside world (*sakoku*). He worshipped his grandfather Tokugawa Ieyasu, and it was he who had Tōshōgū Shrine built.

## Niten-mon

This gate, the biggest at Nikko, is called Niten-mon ("Two-*ten* Gate") because it houses statues of *Jikoku-ten* and *Kōmoku-ten*, two of the four *ten*, the Buddhas who guard the Buddhist faith. It is located half-way up the steps leading into the shrine, and its decorations are concentrated on the upper part so as to provide a beautiful sight from above or below.

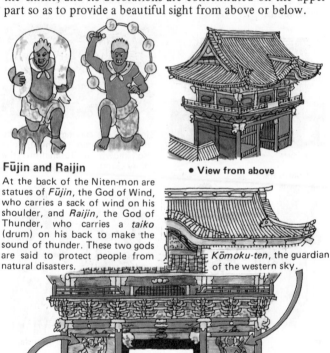

### Fūjin and Raijin

At the back of the Niten-mon are statues of *Fūjin*, the God of Wind, who carries a sack of wind on his shoulder, and *Raijin*, the God of Thunder, who carries a *taiko* (drum) on his back to make the sound of thunder. These two gods are said to protect people from natural disasters.

• View from above

*Kōmoku-ten*, the guardian of the western sky.

*Jikoku-ten*, the guardian of the eastern sky.

• View from below

## Yasha-mon Gate

The Yasha-mon Gate, named after the four statues of *Yasha* at front and back, is Daiyūin-byō's equivalent of Tōshōgū Shrine's Yōmei-mon. Its carvings and coloring are far more simple than those of the elaborate Yōmei-mon, but its gold-based coloring gives it a tone highly suitable for the gate of a mausoleum.

Since all the carvings on the gate consist of *botan* (peonies), it is also known as Botan-mon (the Peony Gate).

**Abatsumara**

**Yasha**  **Bidara**  **Umarokya**  **Gendara**

The name of an Indian god, the word *Yasha* also means "holy and supernatural being". This ugly-looking creature was later adopted as a guardian of Buddhism, and is said to turn into a devil and bring harm to non-believers. Female *Yasha* are said to have the particularly nasty habit of drinking human blood and devouring human flesh.

114

### Kara-mon (Chinese Gate)

The Kara-mon is the smallest gate of the Daiyūin-byō, but its design and decorations are the most elegant. Underneath the *karahafu* gable are a pair of *tsuru* (cranes), and beneath these, a white dragon.

In Japan, cranes (*tsuru*) and turtles (*kamé*) have since ancient times been used in decorations as symbols of longevity, with the crane representing 1000 years and the turtle 10,000. One way of driving away bad luck is said to be to chant repeatedly the words "*tsurukamé, tsurukamé*".

### Shichihengé-no-Momiji

This *momiji*, or maple tree, on the right after the Niten-mon, is called Shichihengé-no-Momiji ("Maple of Seven Changes") because of the way its leaves turn from light to dark green and through shades of yellow and red as the year progresses.

### Soseki

At festivals, *nobori* (banners) are mounted on these stones, of which there are many in the shrine precincts.

Daiyūin-byō has the same layout as Tōshōgū Shrine, with a *hai-den* (worship hall), a *hon-den* (inner shrine) and a connecting chamber known as the Ai-no-Ma, laid out in the shape of a capital H in the *Gongen* style (see p. 69). Brilliantly gilded both inside and out, and richly and intricately carved and decorated, it represents the pinnacle of Edo Era art and craft.

### Hon-den

The Hon-den, constructed in the Chinese *Zenshū* style, houses a seated figure of Tokugawa Iemitsu.

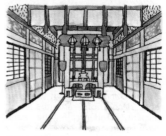

### Ai-no-Ma

This corridor connecting the Hon-den and the Hai-den is the equivalent of Tōshōgū Shrine's Ishi-no-Ma (see p. 70).

With its liberal use of gold leaf and black lacquer, accented with strong color, the interior of the Hon-den is sumptuously and tastefully decorated.

## Kōka-mon

This unusual gate with its Chinese-influenced design is the entrance to the Oku-no-In (Inner Temple), which contains the tomb of Tokugawa Iemitsu. It is also called *Ryūgū-mon* Gate, since its style is imagined to resemble that of Ryūgū-Jō Castle, the castle under the sea where the legendary figure Urashima Tarō was said to have been taken by a grateful turtle.

Ordinary, members of the public are not allowed to enter.

## The legend of Urashima Tarō

The kind-hearted fisherman Urashima Tarō one day bought a baby turtle from some boys who were teasing it on the beach, and released it into the sea. Later, the turtle's mother offered to take him to Ryūgū-Jō, the castle paradise under the sea ruled by Princess Oto-Himé. He accepted the offer and lived a life of luxury in the castle for three years, but finally grew homesick and asked to leave. As a parting gift, the princess gave him a *tamaté-bako*, or treasure casket, but warned him that he must never open it, or dire consequences would follow. On returning to his village, Tarō found that everything had changed and that he no longer recognised any of the people living there. Lonely and depressed, he decided to open the box the princess had given him. As he lifted the lid, white smoke issued forth and Tarō turned in an instant into a venerable white-haired old man.

◆日光博物館

# NIKKO MUSEUM

Nikko Museum *(Nikko Hakubutsukan)* is a reconstruction of the Tamozawa Imperial Villa, which was originally built in 1907. The office and library of this huge villa, which occupies 9,000 m² and has 106 rooms, are preserved in their original state and are open to the public. The museum contains various exhibits and information on the natural history of Nikko.

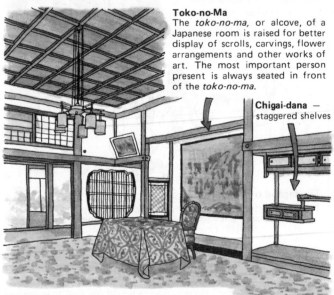

**Toko-no-Ma**
The *toko-no-ma,* or alcove, of a Japanese room is raised for better display of scrolls, carvings, flower arrangements and other works of art. The most important person present is always seated in front of the *toko-no-ma.*

**Chigai-dana —** staggered shelves

**The Audience Hall (Ekken-shitsu)**
The Emperor would receive visitors in this room. A point of interest is that, although the room is designed in the Japanese style, its floor is carpeted and it has Chinese-style windows.

## Sugi-to

The *Sugi-to* are sliding doors made from *sugi* (Japanese cedar). The picture of cockerels is a work of the Momoyama Era (16th century), and the white parts of the painting are done in a mixture of coral and crushed pearls.

## The Library (shosai)

This room is also called *Umé-no-Ma* (the Plum Room) because of the painting of plum trees which decorates one wall. The pillars are made from the wood of the *nanten* tree and there is an unusual circular window.

Nikko Museum presents a plain exterior and conveys a rather relaxed atmosphere considering that it was once an Imperial Villa. The *shidaré-zakura* (weeping cherry) in the garden blossoms beautifully every May even though it is over a hundred years old.

There are many historical sites, rich in legend, in the vicinity of Nikko Museum. These include temples more than three hundred years old, and the Kamman-ga-Fuchi Pool, previously regarded as holy ground after the Buddha *Fudō-Myōō* was said to have appeared there.

**Kamman-ga-Fuchi Pool**
At Kamman-ga-Fuchi, the river flows into a deep pool formed in the lava from Mt. Nantai. The sound of the river is said to resemble an incantation being chanted by *Fudō-Myōō,* and the pool is named after the last word of the incantation, *Kamman.*

**Jiun-ji Temple**
Statues of Amida Nyorai and Jigen Daishi (see p.21) can be seen at this temple, which was built in 1654.

## Kōbō-no Nagefudé

The large Sanskrit characters that can be discerned faintly on the wall of the Kamman-ga-Fuchi Pool are said to have been put there by the priest Kōbō Daishi*, a master of calligraphy, by throwing *(nageru)* his brush *(fudé)* from the opposite bank.

## Narabijizō

The *jizō* (stone images of *Jizō*, or Ksitigarbha, the Buddhist guardian deity of children) facing Kamman-ga-Fuchi Pool are known as *Baké-Jizō* because their number is said to differ depending on the direction in which they are counted.

---

## Water Supply

These stone sisterns are part of the system, made in the Taishō Era, supplying fresh spring water to the former Imperial Villa, Now Nikko Museum.

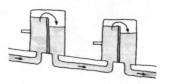

The cisterns are partitioned internally. The water in the front half is used by the house near the cistern, and the overflow fills the back half, from where it is taken by plastic piping to the next cistern.

◆日光江戸村

# NIKKO EDO VILLAGE

Nikko Edo Village, due to open on 23 April, 1986, will be a reconstruction of the life and customs of a typical Edo-Era Village. A visit to this village, with its replicas of *ninja* lodges, local courts, lodging-houses and pleasure quarters, will be like stepping straight back into 18th century Japan. Special plays, films and events will help visitors experience life in the age of the *samurai*.

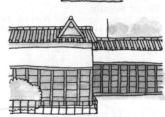

Tōyama-no-Kinsan

### Bugyōsho

The *bugyōsho*, or local magistrate's court, is the setting for many *jidai geki*, or historical dramas. One of the best-known *bugyō* is Tōyama-no-Kin-san, famous for the cherry-tree tattoo on his back.

### Ninja Yashiki

Battles between *samurai* and *ninja* will be re-enacted in the *ninja yashiki (ninja* lodge) with its hidden traps and devices for catching the enemy unawares. Information about the *ninja* and their arts will be displayed in the special exhibition hall.

## Oiran-Dōchū

The *oiran* were the highest class of prostitute in the Edo-Era *yūkaku* (red-light districts). Nikko Edo Village will feature regular re-enactments of the *oiran-dōchū,* the procession in which the gorgeously-kimonoed *oiran,* accompanied by her attendants, proceeds from her quarters to the room where her customer awaits.

Hikifuné — attendant
Oiran

## Shibai-goya

The *shibai-goya,* or playhouse, a reconstruction of an Edo-Era *kabuki* theater, will feature performances of *rakugo* (comic monologs), screenings of historical dramas, and other entertainments.

## Nagaya

The *nagaya* was a wooden 1-storied apartment building with 10 to 20 rooms. Most of the poorer workmen and tradesmen in Edo lived in these apartments, which were small communities whose members would help each other during times of difficulty.

## Yakata-buné

One of the most popular recreational activities of the Edo Era was pleasure boating in the roofed boats known as *yakata-buné.* It will be possible to enjoy this pleasure at Nikko Edo Village as it was in the Edo Era.

## PEOPLE OF THE EDO ERA
## 江戸時代の人々

A rigid caste system known as *Shi-nō-kō-shō* prevailed in the Edo Era. The four main castes were the *bushi,* or *samurai,* who formed the ruling elite; these were followed in order of rank by the *nōmin,* or farmers, the *shokkō,* or artisans, and the *shōnin,* or merchants. The stable political situation allowed the merchants to prosper, however, and they gradually became richer and more powerful. The population of Edo grew to over a million, making it one of the world's biggest cities at that time.

*Chommagé* hairstyle (formal)

**Rōnin**

*Chommagé* hairstyle (imformal)

*Nihon-tō* — Japanese sword

*Kosodé* — undergarment

*Mompuku* — Kimono with family crest

*Kataginu* — formal vest with family crest

*Hakama* — divided skirt

*Zōri* — Japanese sandals

*Geta* — wooden clogs

*Wakizashi* short sword

*Obi* — belt

**Kamishimo style**
(the formal uniform of a *bushi*)

**Kinagashi style**
(the informal style)

## Bushi (Samurai)

The *bushi* class also followed a strict hierarchy, with the *shōgun* at its head. *Bushi* who for one reason or another found themselves with no lord to follow were known as *rōnin,* or "masterless *samurai*", and were usually very poor. These men, the equivalent of the gunmen of America's Wild West, often appear on television or in films as the heroes of the historical dramas known as *jidai-geki.*

# How to make a traditional Japanese hairstyle.

Brush the hair out at the front and keep it separate.

Part the remaining hair down the middle.

Round out at the sides *(bin)* and back *(taba)*.

**Shimada-magé hairstyle**

Brush the front hair back and fasten it.

Form a ring *(magé)* with the middle part.

Women of a *buké (samurai* family) attending a performance of *kabuki.*

## Women of a samurai family

The small-sleeved *kimono* known as *kosodé* were popular, and the patterns on these gradually became bolder and more colorful. Hairstyles went in and out of fashion as they do today.

◆和楽踊り

# WARAKU ODORI

The *Waraku Odori* dance is a *bon* dance performed on 5 and 6 August at the Nikko factory of Furukawa Esectric Co., Ltd. An illuminated *yagura*, or stage, is set up in the center of Waraku pond, and large number of people dance around the outside of the pond, attracting many spectators.

The *Waraku Odori* dance was started to commemorate the first visit of the Imperial family to a Nikko factory. This visit took place in the summer of 1913, when the Imperial household had repaired to Nikko to escape the heat of Tokyo. There are three versions of the dance; *"Te-odori"*, in which the dancers simply wave their arms about while dancing; *"Kasa-odori"*, in which they carry round flowered hats; and *"Ishi-nagé-odori"*, in which they imitate the throwing of stones.

## How to perform Waraku Odori

One

Two

Three

Four

Five

and Six

The *bon* festival, at which the souls of people's ancestors are thought to return to their former homes, ranks with *shōgatsu*\* as one of the most important festivals in Japan. It takes place all over Japan around August 15. Fires called *mukaé-bi* are lit at the start of the festival to guide the dead souls back to this world; they are then offered food and drink, and *bon* dancing for entertainment. At the end of the festival, *okuri-bi* fires are lit to guide them safely back to Heaven.

Horses modeled from eggplants, cucumbers and other vegetables are sometimes placed in front of the houses to provide a means of transport for the dead souls.

One of the best-known *okuri-bi* is Kyoto's Daimonji, one of the *Gosan-okuri-bi*.

### Nikko Yuba

*Yuba* is a protein-rich food made by boiling soybean milk, skimming off the curd that forms on the top, and drying it. The best *yuba* is said to come from Nikko and Kyoto. Nikko Yuba was an important source of protein for the *yamabushi* mountain monks, who were not allowed to eat meat. Many Nikko restaurants serve it.

#### Nama-yuba

Freshly-made *nama-yuba* (raw *yuba*) is often eaten with a dip called *ponzu*, made from vinegar and soy sauce.

#### Agé-yuba no Fukume-ni

To make this dish, *yuba* is fried in oil together with *zemmai* (flowering fern) and *kōya-dōfu* (frozen and dried *tōfu*) and boiled with a light seasoning of salt.

### Shiso-maki Tōgarashi

This spicy, warming food was popular among Nikko's *yamabushi*, mountain priests, and is quite healthy, since it contains no seasonings other than salt. It is prepared by chopping salted *tōgarashi* (chile peppers) finely and wrapping them in *shiso* (beefsteak plant) leaves.

### Jingoro Sembei

*Sembei,* or rice crackers, are made of baked rice flour. Jingoro Sembei are a special type of *sembei* marked with the character *hidari*, meaning left, in memory of Hidari Jingorō, the sculptor who carved the famous Sleeping Cat at Tōshōgu Shrine.

# OKU NIKKO

While Nikko Sannai is renowned for
its shrines and temples,
Oku-Nikko, with Lake Chuzenji at its center,
is famed for its wild natural scenery.
The lakes, rivers, moors, and waterfalls of the area
have a mysterious natural beauty
which changes dramatically with the passing of the seasons.

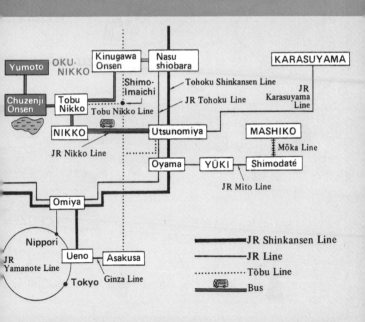

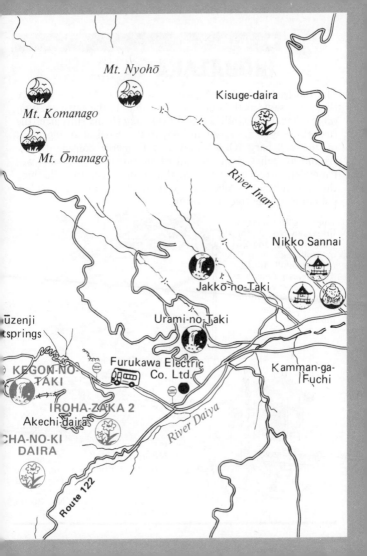

◆いろは坂

# IROHAZAKA

The hill leading to Oku-Nikko has a total of 48 curves. Since this is the same as the number of syllables in the Japanese *hiragana* syllabary, the hill is called *Irohazaka* (Iroha Hill) after the first three syllables *(i, ro* and *ha)* in the classical arrangement of the syllabary. Oku-Nikko was formerly considerd holy ground by believers in the cult of mountain worship, and was banned to women, who were thus prohibited from climbing this hill. It is an excellent place from which to view the splendid colors of the trees in autumn.

There are 20 curves in Irohazaka No. 2, for uphill traffic, and 28 in Irohazaka No. 1, for downhill traffic. The curves are numbered consecutively and each is labeled with a different *hiragana* symbols.

**Nyonin-dō Hall**
Prohibited from climbing to the top of Irohazaka, women would pray to Mt. Nantai from this red-painted hall at bend No. 26 on Irohazaka No. 1.

In the classical arrangement of the *hiragana* syllabary, the *hiragana* are arranged in the form of a poem called *iroha-uta,* with none of the syllables repeated. Nowadays, the *hiragana* syllabary is usually arranged in the systematic, or *a-i-u-e-o,* arrangement, rather than the classical *i-ro-ha* arrangement.

| | | | | | | | |
|---|---|---|---|---|---|---|---|
| い I | ろ Ro | は Ha | に Ni | ほ Ho | へ He | と To | ち Chi |
| り Ri | ぬ Nu | る Ru | を O | わ Wa | か Ka | よ Yo | た Ta |
| れ Re | そ So | つ Tsu | ね Ne | な Na | ら Ra | む Mu | う U |
| ゐ I | の No | お O | く Ku | や Ya | ま Ma | け Ke | ふ Fu |
| こ Ko | え E | て Te | あ A | さ Sa | き Ki | ゆ Yu | め Me |
| み Mi | し Shi | ゑ E | ひ Hi | も Mo | せ Se | す Su | ん N |

(1) **Inu mo arukeba bō ni ataru**
(lit. "Even a dog will find a stick if he takes a walk") Every dog has his day.

(2) **Chiri mo tsumoreba yama to naru**
(lit. "A pile of dust makes a mountain.") Many a little makes a mickle.

(3) **Warenabé ni tojibuta**
(lit. "A cracked lid for a cracked pot") Every Jack must have his Jill.

(4) **Nakittsura ni hachi**
(lit. "Bees to a weeper's face") Misfortunes never come singly.

(5) **Oni ni kanabō**
(lit. "An iron rod for a devil") Making the strong stronger.

## Iroha karuta

*Iroha karuta* is a card game in which half of the 96 cards bear a proverb beginning with a different *hiragana* letter while the other half have matching pictures. The game is to match the proverbs and the pictures. The proverbs differ from region to region.

◆華厳滝

# KEGON-NO-TAKI

Nikko, with its complex topography, has many waterfalls; but the biggest and most beautiful of these is undoubtedly *Kegon-no-Taki*, Kegon Falls, where the River Ōjiri flows swiftly through a 7-m-wide channel over a drop of 97 m. Three tons of water are said to flow over the falls every second, and the pool at the base is 5-m-deep. The falls present a different but equally beautiful face in winter, when they become a cascading chandelier of ice.

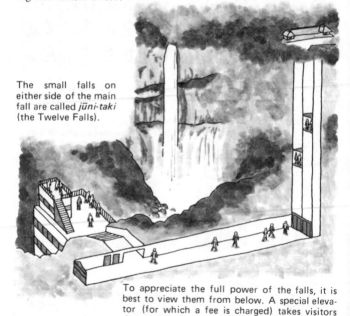

The small falls on either side of the main fall are called *jūni-taki* (the Twelve Falls).

To appreciate the full power of the falls, it is best to view them from below. A special elevator (for which a fee is charged) takes visitors down to a vantage point near the base.

◆茶ノ木平

# CHA-NO-KI DAIRA

A ride to the top of the Chūzen-ji Onsen Cableway brings one to the 1600-m-high Cha-no-ki Daira Hills, from which a wonderful view can be had of Lake Chūzenji, Mt. Nantai, Senjō-ga-Hara and other landmarks. Near the cable-car station is a park where all the alpine flora of Nikko can be seen.

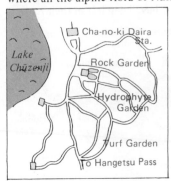

Cha-no-ki Daira Sta.

Lake Chūzenji

Rock Garden

Hydrophyse Garden

Turf Garden

To Hangetsu Pass

A walk in the alpine garden (Kōzan Shokubutsu-en) with its abundant greenery and interesting plants is very relaxing.

## View from Cha-no-ki-Daira

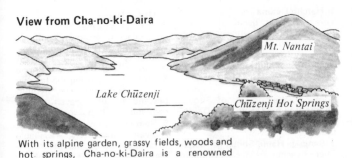

Mt. Nantai

Lake Chūzenji

Chūzenji Hot Springs

With its alpine garden, grassy fields, woods and hot springs, Cha-no-ki-Daira is a renowned beauty spot. A hiking trail leads from here to the Akechi Daira Hills and the Hangetsu Pass.

◆中禅寺湖

# LAKE CHŪZENJI

Lake Chūzenji *(Chūzenji-ko)* was formed when Mt. Nantai erupted and blocked the river Daiya. It has a surface area of 11.5 km² and a periphery measuring 21 km, and is 1269 m above sea level. There are many *ryōkan* and a collection of souvenir shops on the north-east shore, but apart from that, the shores of this beautiful lake have been left in their natural state.

The Japan Amphibian Laboratory

Shōbu-ga-hama

140min.

Semju-ga-hama

30min.

Lake Chūzenji

Futarasan-jinja Chūgu-shi

Iroha-zaka

Kōzuke-jima

Uta-ga-hama

Kegon-no-Taki

Hacchō-dejima

100min.

70min.

Chūzen-ji

Chūzenji Skyline

### 1. Hatchō Dejima
This is the most beautiful area of the lakeside in autumn, when the trees turn color. There is an excellent view from the terrace on the south side of the top of the Hangetsu Pass.

### 2. Kōzuké-Jima
Some of the remains of Shōdō Shōnin (see p.14) and Jigen Daishi (see p.21) are enshrined on this island.

### 3. Senju-ga-Hama Shōbu-ga-Hama
These beaches are lively camping-grounds in summer. A bus goes from here to Yumoto (see p.156).

### 4. Uta-ga-Hama
This quiet and pleasant area is a good place to escape the summer heat, and the British and French embassies have villas here. A legend is told that when Shōdō Shōnin was exploring the lake by boat, a *Tennin* (heavenly nymph) descended from heaven at this spot and sang him a song *(uta)*.

### 5. Boat excursions
A pleasure boat service is available to take visitors to the main sight-seeing spots on the shores of the lake. This service operates from 1 April to 30 November.

**Kegon-no-Taki**  **Lake Chūzenji**

99m

161.5m

62.5m

Lake Chūzenji is extremely deep, with a depth of 125 m in its center and 161.5 m at its deepest part. The bottom is so thick with mud and the pressure so great that the bodies of people drowned in the lake do not rise to the surface.

## The Japan Amphibian Laboratory

This institute, which is open to the public, carries out research into numbers of amphibian creatures, including five varieties of the rare *sanshō-uo* (a large newt-like creature). Some of these amphibians live in Lake Chūzenji.

Besides the beautiful natural scenery, Lake Chūzenji and its environs offer numerous pastimes and amusements, such as camping, hiking and fishing; skiing and skating in winter; and riding in swan- or helicopter-shaped pedal-boats for two. The lake is not really suitable for swimming, however, since it is very cold.

# CHŪZEN-JI TEMPLE

Chūzen-ji Temple and Chūgūshi Shrine were originally at the same spot and were known collectively as Jingū-ji. Chūzen-ji Temple was moved to its present site in 1913, while Chūgūshi Shrine remained where it was. Chūzen-ji Temple is also known as *Tachiki Kannon* after the statue of *Kannon* that it enshrines, which was carved into a living *katsura* tree.

### Hon-dō (Kannon-dō)
The red-painted *hon-dō*, or main hall, where the *Tachiki Kannon* is enshrined, is 11.4 m square and has a *Hōgyō*-style roof*. The steps at the rear lead to the Godai-dō Hall.

### Tachiki Kannon
*Tachiki* means "living tree". This statue is the oldest Buddhist statue at Nikko, and is said to have been carved by Shōdō Shōnin (see p.14) himself after seeing *Senju Kannon* appear above the waters of Lake Chūzenji. It is 5.5 m tall and extends a further 4 m beneath the floor, and has 11 heads, making it a *Jūichimen Senju Kannon*, or "Eleven-faced, thousand-armed Kannon".

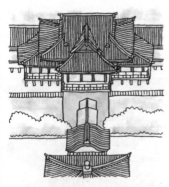

### Godai-dō Hall
The Godai-dō Hall has a railed terrace from which there is an excellent view of Lake Chūzenji.

A large dragon called *Zuiryū* ("auspicious dragon") is painted on the ceiling of the Godai-dō Hall.

The 80 steps from the *hon-dō* lead to the *naijin* (inner sanctuary) of the Godai-dō Hall. *Fudō-Myō-ō* and four other *Myō-ō* (Buddhist guardian deities) are enshrined here.

## Niō-mon Gate

The Niō-mon Gate, the main gate of Chūzen-ji Temple, is named after the two statues of *Niō* (Devas) that guard it. There are two statues, one of *Fūjin,* the god of wind, and one of *Raijin,* the god of thunder, at the rear; and red-lacquered *suki-bei* walls (see p.67) extend on either side.

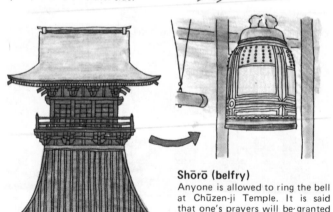

## Shōrō (belfry)

Anyone is allowed to ring the bell at Chūzen-ji Temple. It is said that one's prayers will be granted if one rings the bell slowly three times while praying hard.

### Aizen Myō-ō

The guardian deity of the Aizen-dō Hall, this god has a red face and body and an angry expression. The color red expresses passion, however, and this god is believed to have the power to clear away pain and trouble from relations between the sexes.

### Migawari-no-Kobu

The gnarled excrescence *(kobu)* at the base of this *sugi* (Japanese cedar) tree in the grounds of Chūzen-ji Temple is believed to act as a substitute *(migawari)* for people in accepting their illness and unhappiness.

### Senkō

*Senkō,* the thin sticks of incense offered at Buddhist temples, is available at Chūzen-ji Temple. Light the incense with a candle, fan it with the hand to extinguish the flame (do not blow it out), set the incense in the *senko-taté* (incense stand), and make a wish.

141

◆男体山

# MT. NANTAI

Mt. Nantai, 2,484 m high, is a beautiful conical volcano in the center of the Nikko mountain range. The foothills slope gently down to the town of Nikko, and there is a large 800-m-diameter crater on the north side of the peak. The mountain has been regarded as holy since ancient times and has long been a training-ground for the mountain priests known as *yamabushi*. It is also known as Mt. Futara, or Mt. Fudaraku, the home of Kannon Bosatsu.

### Okumiya

This plain and unadorned shrine, part of the Futarasan Shrine complex, was built by Shōdō Shōnin in 782 in thanks to the gods after he had safely completed his ascent of Mt. Nantai.

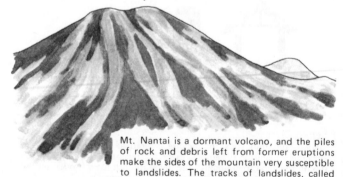

Mt. Nantai is a dormant volcano, and the piles of rock and debris left from former eruptions make the sides of the mountain very susceptible to landslides. The tracks of landslides, called *nagi*, can be seen radiating out from the peak.

### Tarōsan Shrine

This shrine, built on the rocks to the west of the peak of Mt. Nantai, is dedicated to the neighboring mountain, Mt. Tarō. The view of Lake Chūzenji, Senjō-ga-Hara and the surrounding scenery from here is breathtaking.

### Taimen-ishi

Shōdō Shōnin is said to have met with the gods at the point marked by this stone.

Many articles bequeathed as offerings are buried at the summit of Mt. Nantai, which used to be a holy center for the cult of mountain worship.

### Dōkyō

Most of these copper mirrors were cast in the Heian Era* (8th-12th century) and are engraved on the back with flowers and birds.

### Shakujō-gashira

The head of the *shakujō* (staff) of a *yamabushi,* this is an unusual example of such a staff carved in the likeness of a Buddha.

### Kimen

This devil mask, donated in 1537, is meant to keep away evil.

◆中宮祠

# CHŪGŪSHI SHRINE

Chūgūshi Shrine (Central Shrine) is so called because it is located halfway between Futarasan Shrine (See p. 96), in Nikko city center, and Okumiya Shrine (see p. 142), at the top of Mt. Nantai. The path to the summit of Mt. Nantai starts from the back of the shrine grounds, and the shrine has long been known as a base for *tohai,* the climbing of a mountain as an act of prayer.

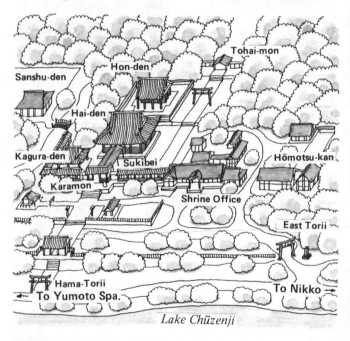

## Tohai-mon Gate

The Tohai-mon is the gate marking the only path to the summit of Mt. Nantai. This path is open from May 5, when the *kaizan-sai,* or "mountain-opening festival", is held, to October 25, when the *heizan-sai,* or "mountain-closing festival" is held.

**Gyōnin Gyōretsu Procession**    **People praying at Okumiya Shrine.**

## Tohai-sai

The *Tohai-sai,* or "mountain prayer festival" is held from late at night on July 3 to August 8. On the first day, three men carry the three statues of the gods enshrined at Chūgūshi Shrine to Okumiya Shrine at the top of Mt. Nantai. After this, the large number of people who have gathered at Chūgūshi Shrine to pray set off from Tohai-mon Gate to climb Mt. Nantai, arriving in time to see the dawn and pray for health and happiness. During the festival, various events take place at Lake Chūzenji (see p. 140).

### Mikoishi

In the days when it was forbidden for women to climb Mt. Nantai, one *miko* (shrine maiden) decided that, since she was a servant of the gods, it would be all right for her to defy the ban. The legend goes that she got as far as Chūgūshi Shrine when she was suddenly turned into this stone, the *Mikoishi*.

### Karamon

The *kaerumata** of the Karamon (Chinese Gate) bear carvings of carp and waves. They are said to have been carved in 1701, but prior to this.

### Hōmotsukan

The museum at Chūgūshi Shrine contains many treasures illustrating Nikko's 1200-year history.

#### Sacred swords

These sacred swords are offered to the gods at the *Yayoi* Festival (see p. 104) on the skin of a male deer.

#### Kondōsō Mikoshi

These gold- and copper-decorated *mikoshi* (portable shrines) were transferred from Futarasan Shrine many years ago.

#### Sanrei Kannō-zu (wall painting)

This picture depicts Shōdō Shōnin and his party about to step onto the summit of Mt. Nantai at the end of the Nara Era. The figures in the painting are facing the Daiya river.

## Praying at a shrine

Throw some money into the *saisen-bako* (collection box) in front of the *hai-den* (worship hall) and ring the bell with the rope attached. The sound of the bell is said to please the gods. Next bow twice, showing your obedience to the gods, and summon them by clapping twice. Pray, and finally bow once more.

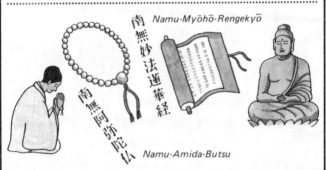

南無妙法蓮華経 *Namu-Myōhō-Rengekyō*

南無阿弥陀仏

*Namu-Amida-Butsu*

## Praying at a temple

Holding a *juzu* (rosary), put the hands together and chant a *nembutsu* (Buddhist invocation) while facing the statue of Buddha. Invocations differ depending on the sect, but the most common ones are "*Namu-Amida-Butsu*", a prayer to *Amida Nyorai*, and "*Namu-Myōhō-Rengekyō*", an invocation to the ancient sutra *Rengékyō*.

# OKU-NIKKO FESTIVALS

The Oku-Nikko area, centered around Lake Chūzenji, retains numerous customs and ceremonies which have their origins in ancient legend. Taking part in these events is a way of becoming aware that Nikko is not merely a sightseeing spot, but a holy area closely connected with Japanese religion.

People stampede along the lakeside road at this festival, hoping to find one of the arrows, since they are thought to act as charms to ward off evil.

### Musha-Matsuri (Jan. 4, Chūgūshi Shrine)

This ceremony originated in the legend in which a great battle was fought among the gods at Senjō-ga-Hara. In this legend, one of Mt. Nantai's allies, the famous archer Sarumaru, pierced the eye of the giant centipede into which Mt. Nantai's enemy, Mt. Akagi, had turned himself. This brilliant shot is now celebrated by shooting arrows in the direction of Mt. Akagi.

## Kojō-sai

This festival, which is related to the Tohai-sai (see p.145), is held on the same day as the latter festival. Those who do not climb Mt. Nantai to pray take Japanese-style boats *(wabuné)* out onto Lake Chūzenji and pray facing the mountain.

Nasu-no-Yoichi

## Ōgi-no-mato Kyūdō Taikai

This festival originates in the story of Nasu-no-Yoichi, one of the Genji* Family generals, and a brilliant archer. He became renowned for his skill at archery after piercing a fan being waved by his enemies on the deck of a ship at the Battle of Yashima *(Yashima-no-Kassen),* the biggest battle between the *Genji* and *Heiké\** families, in 1185. In the festival, arrows are shot at fans *(Ōgi-no-mato)* mounted on boats taken out on Lake Chūzenji.

◆竜頭滝

# RYŪZU-NO-TAKI

These huge falls, which have a total length of 210 m, are to be found on the road leading from Lake Chūzen-ji to Senjō-ga-Hara. The river flows swiftly over black rocks, divides, and falls into two pools. When seen from the front, the water appears to flow in the shape of a dragon's head, leading to the name *Ryūzu-no-Taki* (Dragon's-Head Falls).

The falls are particularly beautiful in May, when the *tsutsuji* (azaleas) bloom, and in October, when the leaves turn red.

A good view of the falls can be had from the viewing terrace near the base. To see all of the falls, walk up the steps on the left-hand bank.

The broad beach on the north shore of Lake Chūzen-ji, called Shōbu-ga-Hama, is a popular camping site in summer because of its beautiful scenery. Near the camping ground are the Nikko fish hatcheries and a teahouse from which there is a fine overall view of Ryūzu Falls.

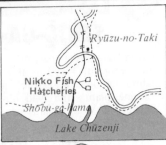

### Semui Dango
The term *semui*, a Buddhist injunction, means "to leave all living creatures in peace". These *dango*, or rice dumplings, come in two varieties; a savory one flavored with soy sauce and a sweet one covered with adzuki-bean jam.

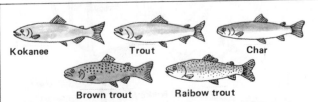

Kokanee    Trout    Char

Brown trout    Raibow trout

### Nikko Fish Hatcheries
The Nikko Fish Hatcheries consist of about 100 pools near Shōbu-ga-Hama where breeding experiments are carried out on various types of fresh-water fish. Anglers can fish for *masu* (rainbow trout) at the hatcheries, and the restaurant serves grilled *masu* and other fish.

◆戦場が原

# SENJŌ-GA-HARA

Senjō-ga-Hara, the marshy moor to the north of Lake Chūzenji, is an average of 1,400 m above sea level. Together with the neighboring Odashiro-ga-Hara, it is a beautiful natural area rich in alpine plants and wild birds. In keeping with its name ("Battlefield Moor"), it is occasionally used as the scene of battles in films.

Senjō-ga-Hara hiking course

## Kōtoku Ranch

Dairy cows are kept at this small ranch, surrounded by woods of silver birch and *zumi,* in the northern part of Senjō-ga-Hara. In winter, it is used for cross-country skiing.

Fresh milk straight from the cow can be bought at Kōtoku Ranch. Other dairy products, ice cream, and cookies are also sold here.

## The Legend of Shinsen (Battle of the Gods)

The name Senjō-ga-Hara comes from the legend according to which Mt. Nantai and Mt. Akagi fought over the rights to the territory. The battle was won by Mt. Nantai, who had turned himself into a giant snake, when his ally Sarumaru shot Mt. Akagi, who had become a huge centipede, in the eye.

**Zumi** — a plant of the rose family, reaching a height of 10 m. Produces white blossoms at the beginning of June.

**Ōakagera** — a variety of *kitsutsuki* (woodpecker) with beautiful black, white and red stripes.

**Akanumafūro** — an alpine plant with charming purple flowers.

**Baikamo** — a kind of algae, this plant produces white flowers resembling plum blossoms.

**Hototogisu** - little cuckoo. The call of this bird is rendered as *"Teppen-Kaketaka"* in Japanese.

**Hozakishimotsuké** — in summer, pink flowers bloom on this plant in the form of ears.

**Rengetsutsuji** — a 1-m-high azalea which produces orange flowers.

**Nikkoazami** — produces thin-stemmed purple flowers. At the end of July, these flowers turn Odashiro-ga-Hara into a mass of purple.

**Himeshakunagé** — a plant of the *tsutsuji* (azalea) family, but resembling the *shakunagé* (alpine rose). Its flowers are bell-shaped and pale purple.

**Rindo** — produces purple bell-shaped flowers in autumn.

**Watasugé** a grass which grows to a length of about 50cm and produces white cotton-like ears.

**Magamo** families of these ducks can be seen on Izumiyado Pond, in the northern part of Senjō-ga-Hara, in June.

**Azuma-Shakunagé** A type of *shakunagé* (alpine rose), this pale red flower blooms from May to June.

**Kisekirei** A type of wagtail with a yellow underside. The throat becomes black in summer.

**Nikko Kisugé** This plant produces beautiful orange lily-like flowers which bloom in the morning and fade away by nightfall.

**Kibitaki** the call of this bird, which resembles the *uguisu,* or Japanese bush warbler, has a clear piccolo-like tone.

**Mahiwa** a sparrow-like bird with beautiful lemon-yellow wings.

**Tsuru Kokémomo** A member of the azalea family, this plant has pink, bell-shaped flowers. Its fruit is edible, thought tart.

**Kakkō** A bird similar to the *hototogisu,* with a call rendered as *"Kakkō, Kakkō".*

155

◆湯元温泉

# YUMOTO HOT SPRINGS

Nikko is a volcanic area, and there are a number of hot springs in its vicinity. One of the best known of these is Yumoto Onsen, discovered in 788 by Shōdō Shōnin. Yumoto has many hotels and guest houses, but most of these are closed from mid-December to mid-March because of the heavy snowfalls in the area. In mid-winter, the temperature can drop to as low as −20°C.

## Lake Yunoko

The mysterious green waters of this lake are the home of water-fowl and trout. With its extensive natural forests, it makes an ideal walking spot.

## Yutaki Falls

These falls are formed from solidified lava. Although the name *Yutaki* means "Hot Water Falls" and *Yunoko* means "Hot Water Lake", the water here is not actually hot, and the falls and lake are only so named because of their proximity to the hot springs. Nearby are a tea-house and an observation deck for viewing the falls.

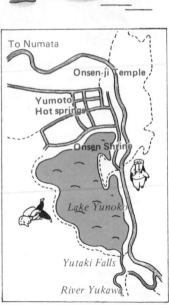

To Numata

Onsen-ji Temple

Yumoto
Hot springs

Onsen Shrine

Lake Yunoko

Yutaki Falls

River Yukawa

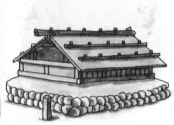

## Onsen Shrine

This shrine, on the high ground to the east of Yumoto Onsen, is dedicated to Mt. Nantai. It used to be combined with Onsen-ji Temple.

**The Source of Yumoto Hot Springs**

The source of the hot springs is the moor behind the town. This water is rich in sulfur and is said to be good for rheumatism, nervous disorders, skin disorders, and external wounds.

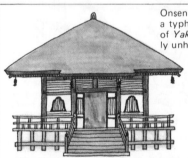

Onsen-ji Temple was destroyed by a typhoon in 1966, but the statue of *Yakushi Nyorai* was miraculously unharmed.

## Onsen-ji Temple

When Shōdō Shōnin discovered Yumoto Onsen in 788, he called the hot water *Yakushi-yu* in dedication to *Yakushi Nyorai,* the Buddha of healing. This was the origin of Onsen-ji Temple. It is possible to bathe in this hot water at the *minshuku* (guest houses) near the temple.

# HOT SPRINGS
## 温泉

Japan is a volcanic archipelago and has innumerable *onsen* (hot springs). Many of these have developed into huge tourist resorts and spas where people go to recuperate from illness, while many remain undeveloped, hidden deep in the mountains and known only to a few people. The water of these springs comes in a variety of colours; springs with a high sulfur content are especially popular.

Wash thoroughly before getting in the bath, and do not use soap or flannel in the bath itself.

### Yukata
The *yukata,* or cotton *kimono,* is actually a sleeping garment, but can also be worn outdoors. It is a particularly common sight in the streets of an *onsen* town.

### Roten-buro (open-air baths)
Open-air rock pools into which the hot water flows and from which the surrounding scenery can be enjoyed while bathing are known as *roten-buro.* Many of these are mixed, unlike public bath-houses, which usually have separate sections for men and women.

# MASHIKO
# YŪKI
# KARASUYAMA

The pottery town of Mashiko,
the silk-weaving town of Yuki,
and the paper-making town of Karasuyama
have been well-known centers for these crafts since ancient times.
As well as buying the products and
observing how they are made here,
it is also possible to try making them oneself.

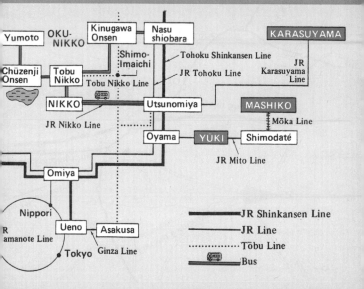

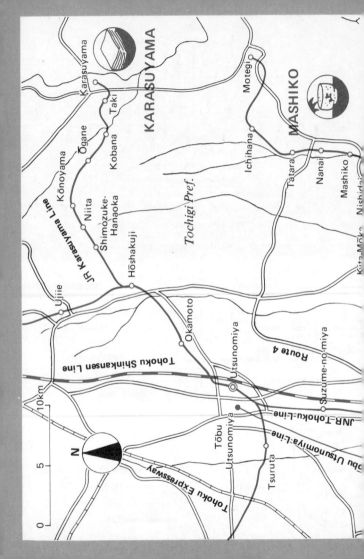

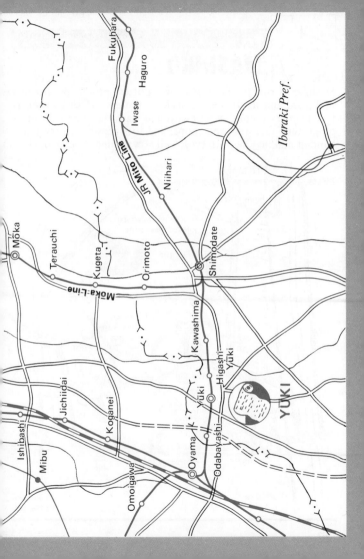

◆益子

# MASHIKO

Mashiko is one of the best-known pottery-producing districts in Japan, and its distinctive style of pottery, *Mashiko-yaki,* is loved for its simplicity, strength and warmth. The town is full of pottery factories and shops, and it is possible to try one's hand at making the pottery as well as watching it being made.

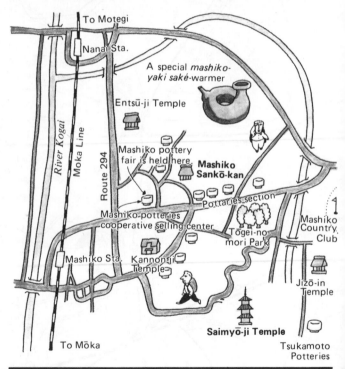

### Saimyō-ji Temple

This old temple, said to have been built in 737, has many Chinese-style buildings, such as the Rō-mon (main gate), Sanjū-no-Tō (three-storied pagoda) and Emma-dō Hall. There is also a huge *hinoki* (cypress) in the grounds that is said to be 700 years old.

### Emma-dō Hall

In this hall is a statue of the King of Hell, *Emma Daiō*, carved in 1714. The statue is unique, since it is the only statue in Japan to depict a god laughing. Beside it are figures representing good and evil.

### The Gion Festival

This festival, Mashiko's version of the Gion Festival of Kyoto (see p.104), is held to drive away disease. It takes place from July 23 - 25, and features a large number of *yatai* (festival floats) with lanterns.

### Omiki Chōdai

In this ceremony held as part of the Gion Festival on July 24, ten people empty a huge red-lacquered dish filled with 6.5ℓ of *saké* three times, in prayer for peace and a good harvest.

## How Mashiko-yaki is made

Unlike many other styles of Japanese pottery, *Mashiko-yaki* is functional and undecorated. However, it is very popular because of its plainness and simplicity.

**(1)**

The clay used in making *Mashiko-yaki* is rich in iron and is not actually very suitable for pottery-making. However, the quality of this clay is what gives *Mashiko-yaki* its distinctive weight and coloring.

**(2)**

The clay is dried and then mixed with water to separate out the dust and sand.

**(3)**

The wet clay is kneaded to remove the last traces of dust and sand and make it workable. If this is not done properly, cracks and imperfections are likely to appear in the final product.

**(4)**

The pot is shaped on the *rokuro* (potter's wheel), which is usually either hand- or foot-driven, and then dried indoors. It is then dried for a week.

**(5)**

Before coloring, the pot is fired at 700 - 800°C to make it better able to absorb the pigment. This firing, called *suyaki,* is omitted with some products.

**(6)**

Pigments containing metals such as iron, copper, manganese and cobalt are used, since they can withstand high temperatures.

**(7)**

The pots are fired in a *nobori-gama,* a series of kilns built one above the other so that the rising heat is not wasted. Red pine is used as the fuel, giving a temperature of 1200 - 1300°C.

**(8)**

The fired pots are allowed to cool for two days before being removed from the kiln. This is the critical moment when the potter finds out whether the firing has been a success or not.

## Mashiko Sankō-kan

The Mashiko pottery museum *(Mashiko Sankō-kan)* exhibits the work of Mashiko's most famous potter, Hamada Shoji, and his collection of foreign pottery, together with the kiln used in making his pots. The building itself is an old Japanese-style house.

**Hamada Shōji**

Hamada Shoji traveled to London with the famous British potter Bernard Leach in 1923 to hold an exhibition of his work, thereby helping to introduce Japanese pottery to the outside world. In 1924, he moved to Mashiko, and helped to perfect the style that characterizes *Mashiko-yaki* today.

Even complete beginners with no experience of potting are welcome at the pottery school, Tsukamoto Potteries.

## Mashiko Pottery Fair

This fair, at which *Mashiko-yaki* can be bought at bargain prices, is held twice a year, from the end of April to the beginning of May and from the end of October to the beginning of November. It usually attracts more than 300,000 people.

It is possible to buy *Mashiko-yaki* directly from the *kamamoto* (pottery makers) in the town, but it may be better to visit some of the larger shops, where a range of different work is on display. There is also a pottery museum featuring pottery from all over Japan, and a pottery school where it is possible to learn every stage of the pottery-making process, from throwing to final firing.

## Japanese Pottery

Pottery, in the form of both works of art and ordinary household utensils, is made in almost every part of Japan except the north. It is usually named after the district where it is made, and has distinct characteristics which depend on the type of clay and manufacturing method used.

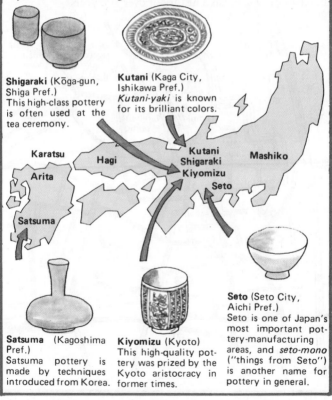

**Shigaraki** (Kōga-gun, Shiga Pref.)
This high-class pottery is often used at the tea ceremony.

**Kutani** (Kaga City, Ishikawa Pref.)
*Kutani-yaki* is known for its brilliant colors.

Karatsu

Hagi

Arita

Kutani
Shigaraki
Kiyomizu

Seto

Mashiko

Satsuma

**Satsuma** (Kagoshima Pref.)
Satsuma pottery is made by techniques introduced from Korea.

**Kiyomizu** (Kyoto)
This high-quality pottery was prized by the Kyoto aristocracy in former times.

**Seto** (Seto City, Aichi Pref.)
Seto is one of Japan's most important pottery-manufacturing areas, and *seto-mono* ("things from Seto") is another name for pottery in general.

◆結城

# YŪKI

The sound of hand looms can still be heard in the town of Yūki, famous for the high-quality woven silk known as *Yūki-tsumugi*. This ancient *jōkamachi* (castle town) with its atmosphere of old Japan has a history of over 800 years.

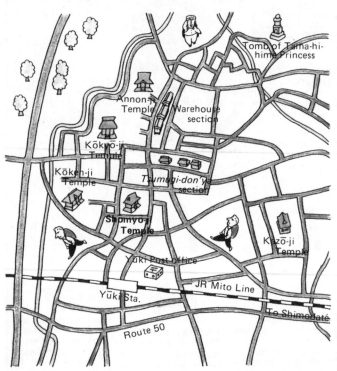

## Teori

*Teori,* Yūki's silk-weaving museum, displays examples of *Yūki-tsumugi* plus exhibits describing its history, together with the tools used in its production. The latter include *izari,* or hand looms.

## Tsumugi-Don'ya

Some of the *ton'ya* (wholesalers) which buy the *Yūki-tsumugi* from the individual producers still have the old-style *chōba,* or reception desks. These wholesalers are known as *tsumugi-don'ya.*

## Shōmyō-ji Temple

Yūki's ruler, Yūki Tomomitsu, built this *Jōdo-shinshu*\* sect temple in 1216. Yūki was often visited by the priest Shinran, the founder of this sect, and there are many memorials to him in the town.

## Kiri-geta

Besides its fame as a producer of *Yūki-tsumugi,* Yūki is also known for its *geta* (clogs), *tansu* (chests) and other products made from *kiri* (paulownia wood). The *geta* made here are prized as top-quality products which greatly enhance the beauty of any *kimono* with which they are worn. These *geta* are all individually hand-made.

*Yūki-tsumugi,* with its distinctive indigo *kasuri* designs, is extremely durable and is used extensively in the manufacture of high-quality *kimono.*

**(1)**

The cocoons are carefully pulled out, and five or six of them are combined into cotton-like pads called *mawata*. The *mawata* are washed in water and allowed to dry in the shade.

**(2)**

The silk thread is then spun from the *mawata* and stored in a wooden tub called *oboké*. It takes a week to make about 80g of thread.

**(3)**

To make the pattern known as *kasuri,* unique to *Yūki-tsumugi,* the thread is tied using hands and mouth. The number of points at which the thread is tied increases with the complexity of the pattern, and this process takes up to a month.

**(4)**

The thread is then dyed with *ai,* an indigo dye made from the powdered *ai,* or Japanese indigo plant, mixed with water, heated to 32 – 33°C over a wood fire and allowed to ferment.

**(5)**

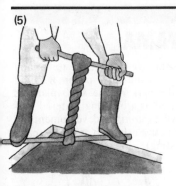

To ensure that the dye thoroughly penetrates the silk, the threads are wound round a stick, banged against a board, and rinsed. This process is repeated twelve times a day for three days.

**(8)**

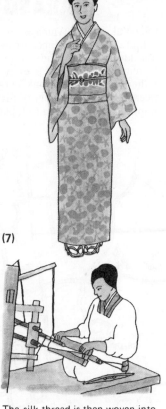

**(6)**

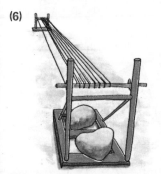

The threads are then aligned to make sure that the pattern is properly matched, then pasted with starch and dried. This is a very important part of the production process and requires great patience.

**(7)**

The silk thread is then woven into cloth on an *izari* hand loom, Japan's oldest type of loom. The highest-quality cloth takes over a year to weave.

◆烏山

# KARASUYAMA

Like Yūki, Karasuyama is an attractive little castle town, and is known as a producer of *washi*, hand-made paper. *Washi*, a translucent paper made from the bark of the *kōzo* plant, is extremely tough and is even used as a building material. Together with the black ink known as *sumi*, its development has given birth to a number of distinctive arts such as *shodō* (calligraphy) and *suibokuga* (ink painting).

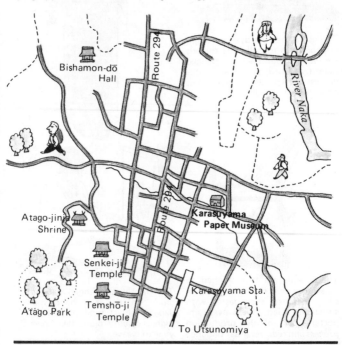

### Ryūmon Falls

These 20-m-high, 65-m-wide falls have two vertical caves in the second stage. The falls are called *Ryūmon* (Dragon's Gate) after a legend in which a dragon is said to have issued from one of the holes.

### Karasuyama Paper Museum

The Karasuyama Paper Museum *(Karasuyama Washi Kaikan)* has exhibits on the history of *washi* and its manufacture and uses. Stationery, dolls and other *washi* products are on sale here.

### Yama-agé-sai

Open-air plays are performed at this festival for warding off illness, held from July 25 to 27. The plays are performed on a 7-m-wide, 10-m-high stage made from bamboo and Karasuyama *washi* and fitted with devices to change the backdrop.

## How Washi is made

Karasuyama *washi* is known for its toughness and excellent texture, and was formerly used for the copying of Buddhist scriptures.

**(1)**

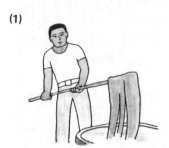

A solution of soda ash is heated in a cast-iron cauldron, and the bark of the *kozo* is boiled for two or three hours in this solution to soften it.

**(2)**

The bark is rinsed in running water, and all dirt and unwanted fiber are carefully removed.

**(3)**

The bark is then placed on a board made of *kashi* (oak) and beaten with an oak stick to separate out the fibers.

**(4)**

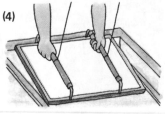

The fibers are then placed in a tub containing water and starch, mixed with a stick, and scooped up in a bamboo frame through which the water is allowed to drain, leaving an even layer of paste. The left-right, back-and-forth motion of this process, known as *kamisuki,* is unique to *washi*-making.

**(5)**

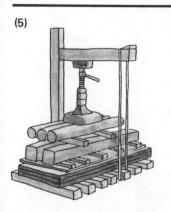

The wet paper is placed in a press and the water is slowly squeezed out over a period of 7 -8 hours.

**(6)**

The individual sheets are then laid out on boards and dried. As well as seeing *washi* made, it is also possible at Karasuyama to try making it oneself.

**(7)**

*Washi* is used to make small chests of drawers, kites, wallets, dolls, decorations and other handicrafts as well as being used for notepaper.

Ichigai, in south Karasuyama, specializes in making the bold, *sumi*-based paintings of *shōgun* known as *musha-é* ("warrior paintings"). These can be seen on the *nobori* (banners) which people place outside their houses at the *Tango-no-Sekku* (Boys' Day) festival on May 5 in prayer that their children will grow up strong and healthy.

# HISTORICAL TABLE

| C. | Era | Japan (Nikko) | World |
|---|---|---|---|
| 6 | Asuka Era | | 502 Byzantine Empire and Persia at war. |
| | | | 527 Justinian I ascends to the throne. Height of Byzantine Empire. |
| 7 | | 538 Buddhism introduced to Japan | 622 Islam founded by Mahomet. |
| | | | 634 Islamic Jihad begins. |
| 8 | Nara Era | 710 Capital moved to Nara (Heijō-kyō) | 711 Saracen army invades Spain. |
| | | 766 Shihonryū-ji Temple built (p.18). | 768 Carl ascends to French throne. |
| | | 782 Shōdō Shōnin climbs Mt. Nantai. | |
| | | 784 Chūzen-ji Temple built (p.138). | |
| | | 790 Futarasan Shrine built at site of present Hongū Shrine (p.96). | |
| 9 | Heian Era | 794 Capital moved to Kyoto (Heian-kyō). | 800 Roman Empire flourishes. |
| | | 805 Tendai-shū sect introduced by Saichō. | |
| | | 806 Shingon-shū sect introduced by Kūkai. | 829 Edward of Essex unites England. |
| | | 848 Rinnō-ji Temple built (p.20). Jōgyō-dō Hall and Hokké-dō Hall built (p.106). Nikko becomes | |
| 10 | | sacred to Tendai-shū sect. | 936 Otto becomes Emperor of Germany. |
| | | | 962 Holy Roman Empire established. |
| 11 | | | 1054 Partition of Greek and Roman churches. |
| 12 | | | 1096 First Crusade. |
| | | 1159 Heiké family seizes power. | |

| C. | Era | Japan (Nikko) | World |
|---|---|---|---|
| 13 | Kamakura Era | 1185 Heiké family ousted by Genji family.<br>1192 Kamakura Shogunate established.<br>**1210 Shugendō started at Nikko (p.32).**<br>**1215 Futarasan Shrine moved to present site.** | 1198 Innocentus III becomes Pope. |
| 14 | Namboku-cho Era | 1333 Kamakura Shogunate collapses. | |
| | Muromachi Era | 1336 Muromachi Shogunate established at Kyoto. | 1339 England and France start One Hundred Years' War.<br>1347 Plague sweeps Europe. |
| 15 | | | 1429 Joan of Arc breaks siege of Orleans.<br>1453 Fall of Byzantine Empire. |
| | | 1467 Battle of Ōnin fought for succession to Muromachi Shogunate. Beginning of Warring States Era. | 1455 England's Wars of the Roses begin.<br>1480 Ivan III lays foundation for Russian Empire.<br>1492 Discovery of America by Columbus. |
| 16 | | | 1517 Protestant Reformation begun by Martin Luther. |
| | Azuchi Momoyama Era | 1549 Christianity introduced by Spanish missionaries.<br>1573 Collapse of Muromachi Shogunate. Oda Nobunaga seizes power.<br>1582 Oda Nobunaga killed. Toyotomi Hideyoshi succeeds as ruler of Japan. | 1522 Magellan circles the globe.<br>1588 Spanish Armada defeated by English Navy. |

| C. | Era | Japan (Nikko) | World |
|---|---|---|---|
| 17 | Edo Era | 1600 Battle of Seki-ga-Hara. Tokugawa Ieyasu battles with the Toyotomi family for control of Japan. <br> 1603 Tokugawa Ieyasu establishes Edo (present-day Tokyo) Shogunate. <br> 1613 Christianity prohibited. <br> 1616 Tokugawa Ieyasu dies. <br> **1617 Tōshōgū Shrine built. (p.33)** <br><br> **1634 Tokugawa Iemitsu starts grand rebuilding of Tōshōgū Shrine.** <br> 1637 Battle of Shimabara (Christian uprising) <br> 1639 Japan closed to outside world. <br><br> **1650 Gojū-no-Tō built at Tōshōgū Shrine (p.40).** <br> 1651 Tokugawa Iemitsu dies. <br> **1653 Daiyūin-byō completed (p.110).** <br><br> 1680 Tokugawa Tsunayoshi becomes 5th Shōgun. | 1618 Thirty Years' War begins in Germany. <br> 1620 British Pilgrims depart for New World in Mayflower. <br><br><br> 1642 English Puritan Revolution. <br> 1643 Louis XIV succeeds to French throne. <br> 1649 Cromwell establishes republic in England. <br><br> 1660 English Restoration <br><br> 1688 Bloodless Revolution <br> 1689 Peter becomes King of Russia. <br> 1702 Queen Anne War |
| 18 | | 1721 Tokugawa Yoshimuné becomes 8th Shōgun. | |

| C. | Era | Japan (Nikko) | World |
|---|---|---|---|
| 19 | Edo Era | | 1763 Britain colonizes India and Canada. Industrial Revolution begins.<br>1775 American War of Independence begins.<br>1789 French Revolution<br>1804 Napoleon becomes Emperor of France.<br>1840 Opium Wars<br>1848 French February Revolution. German March Revolution. California Gold Rush.<br>1861 American Civil War begins.<br>1871 Germany unified under Kaiser Wilhelm I. Paris commune. |
| | Meiji Era | 1853 American Navy forces Japan to break its self-imposed isolation.<br>1867 Meiji Restoration. Emperor's forces wrest power from 15th Shōgun Tokugawa Yoshinobu.<br>**1890 JNR Nikko Line starts operation.**<br>1904 Japan and Russia War.<br>**1913 Chūzen-ji Temple moved to present site. (p. 138)** | |
| 20 | Taisho Era<br><br>Showa Era | 1914 First World War starts.<br>**1929 Tōbu Nikko Line starts Operation.**<br>**1934 Nikko becomes National Park.**<br>1941 Japan attacks Pearl Harbor. Pacific War begins.<br>1945 Atomic bomb falls on Hiroshima. Japan surrenders unconditionally.<br>1964 Tokyo Olympics held. Japan's economic growth begins.<br>**1972 Lake Chūzenji Skyline Highway opened.** | 1914 First World War begins.<br>1917 Russian Revolution<br>1929 Great Depression.<br>1933 Hitler controls Germany.<br>1939 Second World War begins. |

# GLOSSARY

**Amida Nyorai** 阿弥陀如来
The Buddha revered by the Jōdo-shū and Jōdoshin-shū sects. He taught that those who chanted the refrain "Namu-Amidabutsu" would go to the Buddhist heaven after their death.

**Azuchi-Momoyama Era (1573 — 1598)** 安土桃山時代
The era after the Sengoku (Warring States) Era when Japan once again became a united country. Known for its ornate arts and crafts.

**Bosatsu** 菩薩
A Bodhisattva, or living Buddha (see p.79).

**Chadō** 茶道
The tea ceremony, a code of etiquette used when serving *nihoncha* (green tea) to guests. Influenced by *zen,* it attemps to create a world of harmony and tranquillity.

**Edo Era (1603 — 1867)** 江戸時代
An age of great political stability in which Japan was controlled by the *shōgun,* starting with Tokugawa Ieyasu.

**Fudō-myō-ō** 不動明王
Fudō-myō-ō depicts *Dainichi-nyorai* (the sun become Buddha) with an angry expression, destroying evil spirits and earthly passions. He is usually depicted sitting on a stone amid a mass of flames.

**Gagaku** 雅楽
Ancient court music from the seventh century, used as an accompaniment to *kagura* (see p.65).

**Goma** 護摩
Sacred fire used in ceremonies by *yamabushi* (mountain priests) to purify the area and drive away evil spirits.

**Heian Era (794 — 1191)** 平安時代
An era when the aristocracy flourished, creating its own refined form of culture, and Kyoto was the capital of Japan.

### The Hōgyō-zukuri 方形造り

A type of roof-style in which the roof is square and is decorated with a metal ball called a *hōju* at its peak (see p.77).

### The Irimoya Style 入母屋造り

A combination of the *Kiritsuma* and *Yosemuné* styles. (see p.77)

### Jūnishi 十二支

Consists of 12 year cycles, with each year in the series named after a different creature (rat, ox, tiger, rabbit, dragon, serpent, horse, sheep, monkey, cock, dog, wild boar – in Japanese, *ne, ushi, tora, u, tatsu, mi, uma, hitsuji, saru, tori, inu, i*). These 12 signs are called *jūni-shi.* They are usually used in conjunction with ten calendar signs called *jikkan,* and the total zodiac system thus contructed, the calculation of which is extremely complex, is called *eto.* It is closely related to the 12 Western zodiac signs.

### Kabuki 歌舞伎

One of Japan's best-known performing arts, at first performed only by women, but now only by men. It is characterized by its gorgeous costumes, strange makeup and elaborate sets.

### Kaerumata 蟇股

The assembly used to support the roof in traditional Japanese buildings, constructed without nails.

### Kagura 神楽

Sacred dance and music performed in homage to the gods. Said to have originated in the dance performed at *Iwato biraki.* (See p.65)

### (Iwato-biraki)

According to legend, the world became dark when the sun god, *Amaterasu Ōminokami,* hid herself in a cave. To lure her out, a beautiful female goddess was said to have danced in front of the cave.

### Kamakura Era (1192 – 1333) 鎌倉時代

The era in which the seat of government was located at Kamakura, near present-day Tokyo. The great *samurai* families, starting with the Genji* family and followed by the Hōjō family, controlled the country during this era, which was also known for its large number of new Buddhist sects.

**Kannon** 観音

A *Bosatsu* regarded by large numbers of believers as the savior of the world.

**Kara-hafu** 唐破風

An arch-shaped gable used to decorate a roof (see p.77).

**Kiritsuma-zukuri** 切妻造り

The most orthodox type of roof style, in which the roof is divided longitudinally by a single central ridge (see p.77).

**Kūkai (774 — 835)** 空海

Founder of the Shingon-shū Sect.

**Mikoshi** 神輿

A kind of portable shrine into which a god descends at festivals.

**Minamoto-no-Yoritomo** 源頼朝

The founder of the Kamakura Shogunate; the first military commander to assume political power in Japan.

**Momoyama Era (1573 — 1602)** 桃山時代

The Azuchi-Momoyama Era is divided into two periods: the Azuchi Era, in which Oda Nobunaga was Shōgun, and the Momoyama Era, in which Toyotomi Hideyoshi was Shōgun.

**Nagaré-zukuri** 流造り

A type of shrine architecture in which the roofs are designed with one side greatly elongated (see p.77).

**Nara Era (710 — 784)** 奈良時代

The era in which Nara was the capital of Japan, an era in which many huge Buddhist temples were constructed.

**Oda Nobunaga (1534 — 1582)** 織田信長

A brake general who survived the Warring States Era and reunited Japan.

**Samurai** 侍

A generic term used to describe the warrior class, or *samurai*, until modern times. Japan was controlled by *bushi* for eight centuries, starting in the 11th century.

**Sengoku Era (1477 — 1573)** 戦国時代

The Warring States Era, in which Japan was divided into a large number of separate states. This era came to an end when Japan was reunited by Toyotomi Hideyoshi.

**Senju Kannon** 千手観音

A thousand-armed, thousand-eyed *Kannon*.

**The Shingon-shū sect (Heian Era)** 真言宗

This sect, founded by Kūkai, teaches the mystic doctrine that by chanting *shingon* (words of truth) and entering into a spirit of Buddhahood, it is possible to become a living Buddha.

**Shintō** 神道

Japan's indigenous religion, akin to animism and deifying the Emperor.

**Shōgatsu** 正月

New Year's Day, the most important of the year, when various ceremonies are carried out to pray for happiness and prosperity in the year to come.

**Shōgun** 将軍

In the olden days, this was the highest military rank. It became the usual term for the ruler of Japan when the country changed to a military state in the Kamakura Era.

**Sugawara Michizané (845 — 903)** 菅原道真

A renowned scholar of the early Heian Era.

**The Tendai-shū sect (Heian Era)** 天台宗

This sect bases its teachings on a holy scripture called *Hokekyō*, said to be the most mystical of all the Buddhist doctrines. The sect was introduced into Japan by the priest Saichō and was the precursor of the *Zen, Jōdo* and *Nichiren* sects.

**Toyotomi Hideyoshi (1536 — 1598)** 豊臣秀吉

The military commander who took over from Oda Nobunaga in the work of unifying Japan (see p.61).

**The Zen sect (Kamakura Era)** 禅宗

*Zen* is a form of Buddhist training in which the acolytes bring themselves through meditation to the point where they are capable of receiving instant enlightenment. The *Zen* sect regards this as the most important form of training, and places more emphasis on individual enlightenment than on the salvation of the people as a whole.

# INDEX